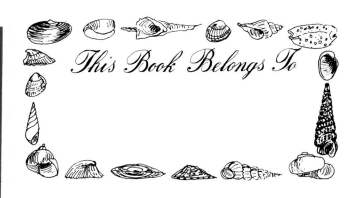

This Book Belongs To

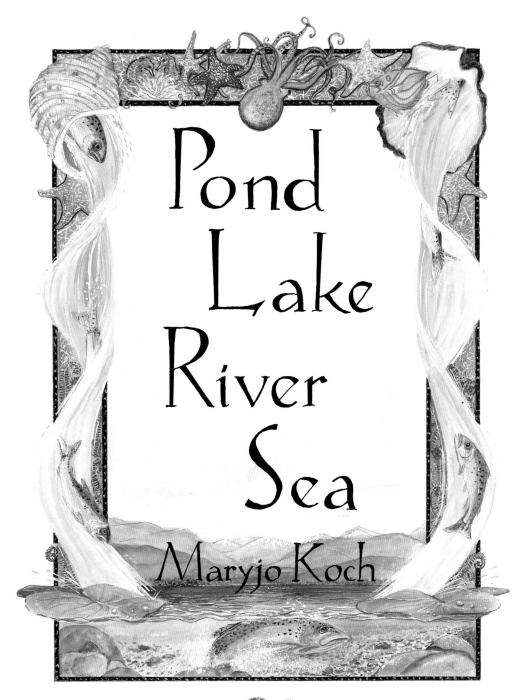

Pond
Lake
River
Sea

Maryjo Koch

SWANS ISLAND BOOKS

SMITHMARK

THIS EDITION PUBLISHED IN 1998 BY SMITHMARK PUBLISHERS, A DIVISION OF U.S. MEDIA HOLDINGS, INC.,
115 WEST 18TH STREET, NEW YORK, NY 10011.

SMITHMARK BOOKS ARE AVAILABLE FOR BULK PURCHASE FOR SALES PROMOTION AND PREMIUM USE. FOR
DETAILS WRITE OR CALL THE MANAGER OF SPECIAL SALES, SMITHMARK PUBLISHERS, 115 WEST 18TH STREET,
NEW YORK, NY 10011; (212) 519-1300.

PUBLISHED IN 1994 BY COLLINS PUBLISHERS SAN FRANCISCO, 1160 BATTERY STREET, SAN FRANCISCO, CA 94111

A SWANS ISLAND BOOK

LIBRARY OF CONGRESS CATALOG CARD NUMBER: 98-60009

ISBN 0-7651-0760-0

PRINTED IN HONG KONG
10 9 8 7 6 5 4 3 2 1

In memory of my father
Henry Charles Moeller

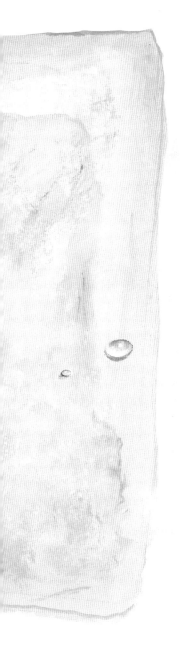

"*Life bears the memory of its aquatic origins. Every living creature, animal or plant ... even man ... is above all a form of water.*"

JEAN DORST, <u>WATER</u>, 1990

Technology
has finally permitted us some real intimacy
with marine life, but much of that world beneath
the blue mantle still remains shrouded in mystery.

The western ancients saw the god
Poseidon (or Neptune) commanding the seven seas with a flourish
of his Olympian trident. They believed sea nymphs and mermaids
lingered upon lonely rocks along the shore, combing their tresses with
the long spines of Murex shells and seducing unsuspecting sailors.

Eastern legends from Babylonia, India,
China, and Japan bring us tales of the Dragon Kings, who zealously
guarded their treasures of gems and pearls in palaces at the
bottom of the sea.

Aphrodite (or Venus), the classical goddess
of love, was born fully formed from the sea foam. As she rose
from the waves on a shell, droplets of water fell back into the sea
and hardened into pearls, the embodiment of her sensual charms.

The fisher king of Christian legend
served as keeper of the Holy Grail. He was crippled, and fishing
was his only pastime.

Pisces, the astrological sign of the
two fishes, is the sun sign ruled by the planet Neptune. It is said
that Pisceans thrive in the watery domain of the emotions.

Fish, as well as many mollusks, have
been considered holy food, brain food, fertility symbols,
aphrodisiacs, weather forecasters, and an essential part of potions,
charms, and magic spells. In ancient Egypt the fish
deity Rem fertilized the land with his tears.
The Celts imbued fish with the
sacred power of
foreknowledge.

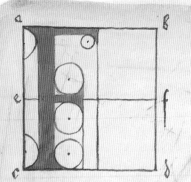

THE KINDS OF FISH ARE AS UNLIKE EACH OTHER AS THE FOUR CLASSES OF AIR-BREATHING ANIMALS, WHICH ARE: AMPHIBIANS, REPTILES, BIRDS, AND MAMMALS. DESPITE THE MIND-BOGGLING VARIETY OF HABITS, FORMS, SIZES AND COLORS, HOWEVER, FISH DO HAVE A FEW CHARACTERISTICS IN COMMON: MOST HAVE SOME VERSION OF BONY SKELETON, SKIN WITH SCALES, AND GILLS.

UNTIL 1938 SCIENTISTS BELIEVED THE COELACANTH, A BONY FISH, DIED OUT 80 MILLION YEARS AGO. THEN THEY DISCOVERED THE CREATURE ALIVE AND WELL OFF THE COAST OF SOUTH AFRICA. SHOULD YOU GET A FLAT TIRE WHILE BICYCLING IN THAT AREA LOCALS WILL SHOW YOU HOW TO ROUGH UP THE INNER TUBE WITH A COELACANTH SCALE BEFORE APPLYING A PATCH.

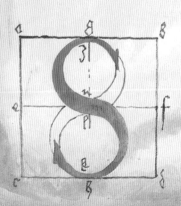

FISCHE PESCE VIS

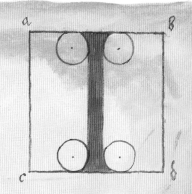

LIVING FISH FIT INTO THREE MAJOR CLASSES. THE FIRST OF THESE ARE THE JAWLESS FISHES SUCH AS LIKE LAMPREYS AND HAGFISH, A TOTAL OF ABOUT 45 SPECIES. THE CARTILAGINOUS FISHES, WHICH INCLUDE SHARKS, RAYS, AND SKATES, NUMBER ABOUT 600 SPECIES. AND THE BIGGEST GROUP, ENCOMPASSING MORE THAN 25,000 SPECIES, ARE THE BONY FISHES, SUCH AS LUNGFISH, EELS, STURGEON, GAR, PERCH, AND CARP JUST TO NAME A FEW.

WHEN IT COMES TO FISH, THE RANGE IN SIZE IS INCREDIBLE. THE DWARF PYGMY GOBY, A FRESH WATER RESIDENT OF THE PHILIPPINES, CAN MEASURE LESS THAN 0.3 INCHES LONG WHEN FULLY GROWN. AT THE OPPOSITE END OF THE SPECTRUM, THE PLACID, PLANKTON-FEEDING WHALE SHARK CAN EASILY GROW TO MORE THAN 60 FEET LONG AND TIP THE SCALES AT 5 BILLION TIMES THE WEIGHT OF THE DIMINUTIVE GOBY.

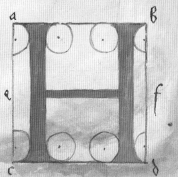

SAKANA FISH

THE PRIMORDIAL SOUP

LIFE ON EARTH EMERGED FROM THE PRIMORDIAL SOUP OF THE ANCIENT SEAS, A WATER WORLD THAT PULSED WITH ALL THE ENERGY AND CREATIVITY OF NATURE. EVER SINCE, INFINITE VARIETY HAS DEFINED THIS REALM OF NEAR-ZERO GRAVITY AND CONTINUAL CHANGE.

NATURE HAS HAD PLENTY OF TIME TO EXPERIMENT IN THE OCEANS. SCIENTISTS TENTATIVELY DATE THE EARLIEST UNDERSEA LIFE TO THE PRECAMBIAN ERA, SOME 4 BILLION YEARS AGO. FOR 2 BILLION YEARS, BACTERIA AND FILAMENTOUS BLUE-GREEN ALGAE ACCOUNTED FOR MOST LIFE ON EARTH. THROUGH THE ALCHEMY OF PHOTOSYNTHESIS THESE MIGHTY MICROBES GENERATED OUR OXYGEN-RICH ATMOSPHERE.

TODAY THE DESCENDANTS OF THE FIRST SEA DWELLERS SURVIVE BASICALLY UNALTERED FROM THE ORIGINAL DESIGN. THESE STROMATOLITES ARE LIKE LOST COLONIES OF LIVING FOSSILS TRAPPED IN THE SEDIMENT AND ALGAE OF AUSTRALIA'S SHARK BAY.

LIFE CONTINUED ITS SINGLE CELL MONOTONY FOR MANY HUNDREDS OF MILLIONS OF YEARS UNTIL THE SEXUAL REVOLUTION MADE NATURAL SELECTION POSSIBLE. GENETIC VARIATION BROUGHT BIOLOGICAL DIVERSIFICATION. NEW SPECIES APPEARED: FIRST THE HERBIVORES AND THEN THE VORACIOUS CARNIVORES.

FROM THIS COALITION OF TINY CREATURES, COMPLEX MULTI-CELLED SPONGES MATERIALIZED ONE BILLION YEARS AGO. ARMED TO DEFEND THEMSELVES AGAINST PREDATORS, THEY LAUNCHED THE EVOLUTIONARY ARMS RACE.

THE ARRIVAL OF THE SPONGES HERALDED THE START OF THE "CAMBRIAN EXPLOSION", WHEN THOUSANDS OF MULTI-CELLED LIFE FORMS BURST ONTO THE SCENE.

FISH, TODAY'S MASTER MARINERS, WERE JOHNNY-COME-LATELIES, SWIMMING INTO THE PICTURE ONLY AFTER ANOTHER 20 MILLION YEARS OR SO.

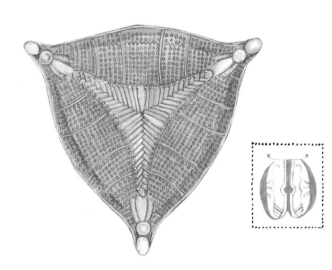

WHO'S WHO IN THE HABITAT?

But what an endless work have I in hand
To count the sea's abundant progeny
Whose fruitful seeds farre passeth those on land.
— EDMUND SPENSER

In 1909 paleontologist Charles Walcott found an unprecedented deposit of marine fossils in the Burgess Shale of British Columbia, Canada. Recent reconstructions of this fossil evidence indicate that after the "Cambrian Explosion" a great variety of basic body plans, or phylums, existed in the oceans (though the diversity amongst species was less than today). Then, mysterious and random global cataclysms ravaged these flourishing communities. The late Permian event of 225 million years ago — the granddaddy of all catastrophes — extinguished 96 percent of all marine species.

Today we live with the survivors in the Holocene epoch, which began 1.5 million years ago.

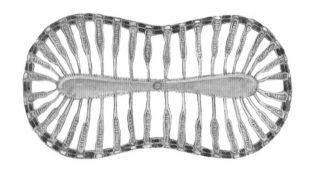

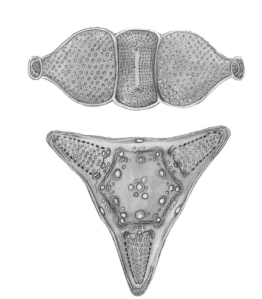

Plankton

Minute wanderers called plankton drift through the upper waters of the ponds, lakes, rivers and seas that cover two thirds of our planet.

These industrious microbeasts utilize solar energy to extract minerals from the water, perform photosynthesis, store the resulting carbohydrates and release, as a by-product, nearly 80 percent of the earth's oxygen supply.

The single-celled overachievers form the first link of the vast global food chain. Undaunted by environmental extremes — even in the frigid polar regions — plankton float passively throughout the world's water. They are the food of choice for krill, miniscule shrimp-like creatures that sustain the mammoth baleen whales.

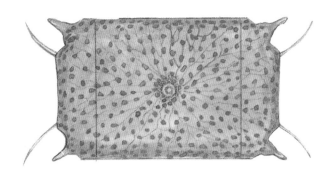

Porifera and Coelenterata

Taxonomy is so taxing! What can lifeforms as diverse in appearance as corals, anemones and jellyfish have in common? Introduce yourself to one of the 9000 species of the phylum Coelenterata just before its lunchtime and find out. The round, symmetrical critter will invitingly reach out to you with flexible and contractible arms, loaded with stinging cells called nematocysts. Stunned or worse, you'll realize that luncheon is being served -- and you're it!

Mature sponges, of the phylum Porifera (10,000 species), and some coelenterates such as corals and anemones are permanently attached to one spot and cannot move. They ingratiate themselves to their neighbors through acts of hospitality. For those they have deemed compatible or inedible, they willingly provide lodgings in their numerous tubes and canals.

Corals have outpaced sponges as the dominant reef builders, but sponges dutifully keep the place fresh. Living vacuum cleaners, they filter 99 percent of all bacteria out of the water. A teacup-sized sponge will filter about 1,250 gallons a day, processing its own volume every 4 to 20 seconds. Perhaps this is one explanation for the crystalline waters near tropical reefs.

Mollusks

All 80 to 100 thousand mollusk species share the distinguishing feature of the mantle: not a perch for bric-a-brac above your fireplace but the miraculous membrane that creates the lustrous seashells you put there.

The mantle surrounds the mollusk's soft body parts. Within its middle fold nestles the sensory perception system and any tentacles the creature might have. At its outermost folded margin, it creates a shell if the creature has one. Certain mollusks, like the oyster, can produce one of nature's most dazzling accomplishments, the pearl.

The nimble, intelligent octopus, a mollusk without a shell, has eyes as sophisticated as most mammals. Meanwhile, the chiton, the armadillo of the seas, can have up to 12,000 microscopic eyespots embedded in the surface of its shell.

ECHINODERMS

STARFISH ARE THE GOODWILL AMBASSADORS OF THE 6,000 SPECIES OF SPINY-SKINNED, HYDRAULICALLY OPERATED MARINE INVERTEBRATES KNOWN AS ECHINODERMS. SEEN THROUGH THE WATERS OF A TIDE POOL, WASHED UP ON THE SHORE OR CLINGING TO A REEF, THEIR WHIMSICAL FORM AND CHARMING VARIATIONS DISTRACT US FROM THEIR DANGEROUS NEXT OF KIN: SEA URCHINS, THE LIVING PIN CUSHIONS WITH TOXIC TINES.

A STARTLING FEAT OF THIS PHYLUM IS REGENERATION. MOST ECHINODERMS CAN RENEW AT LEAST AN ARM; MANY CAN REPLACE UP TO HALF THEIR BODIES. BUT THE DOUGHTY SEA CUCUMBER WINS IN THIS CATEGORY: WHEN FRIGHTENED IT VIOLENTLY CONTRACTS ITS SAUSAGE-SHAPED BODY AND EXPELLS A TANGLED MASS OF INTERNAL ORGANS. AFTER A FEW WEEKS IN HIDING IT IS BACK IN ACTION ON THE SEA FLOOR, EQUIPPED WITH ENTIRELY NEW INSIDES.

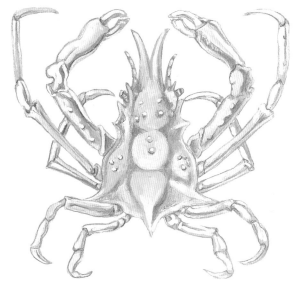

CRUSTACEANS

IN THE NUMBERS GAME OF BIODIVERSITY CRUSTACEANS PERFORM WELL, WITH 39,000 SPECIES DIVIDED INTO 10 CLASSES. REMINISCENT OF INSECTS, WITH THEIR PAIRED ANTENNAE, JOINTED LIMBS, AND SEGMENTED EXOSKELETONS, THEY HAVE ADAPTED TO MOST MARINE HABITATS AND MANY FRESHWATER ONES.

RANGING IN COLOR FROM TRANSPARENT TO PSYCHEDELIC, SHRIMP, CRABS AND LOBSTERS OFTEN LIVE IN HIDING, AS THEY MAKE A SUCCULENT MEAL FOR AQUATIC PREDATORS. THE RETIRING ARTHROPODS ARE PARTICULARLY VULNERABLE DURING GROWTH SPURTS, WHEN THEY MOLT, CASTING OFF THEIR CHITINOUS ARMOR. DELECTABLE AND SWEET, THE SOFT-SHELLED CRAB IS, IN FACT, AN UNFORTUNATE CRUSTACEAN CAUGHT WITHOUT ITS SHIRT ON!

OND

"Fish say they have their stream and pond;
But is there anything beyond?
And in that Heaven of all their wish,
There shall be no more land say fish."

RUPERT BROOKE, <u>HEAVEN</u>, 1913

"*In the end,*

we will conserve only what we love,

we will love only what we understand,

. we will understand only what we are taught."

— BABA DIOUM, SENEGALESE CONSERVATIONIST

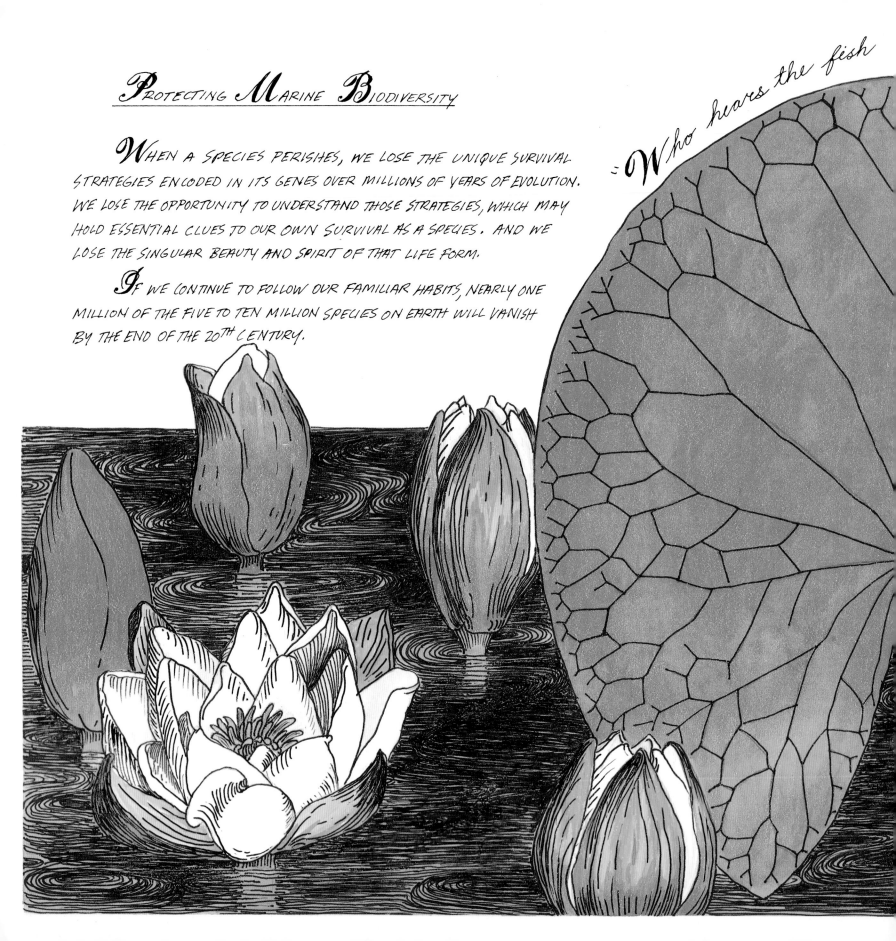

Protecting Marine Biodiversity

When a species perishes, we lose the unique survival strategies encoded in its genes over millions of years of evolution. We lose the opportunity to understand those strategies, which may hold essential clues to our own survival as a species. And we lose the singular beauty and spirit of that life form.

If we continue to follow our familiar habits, nearly one million of the five to ten million species on earth will vanish by the end of the 20th century.

"Who hears the fish

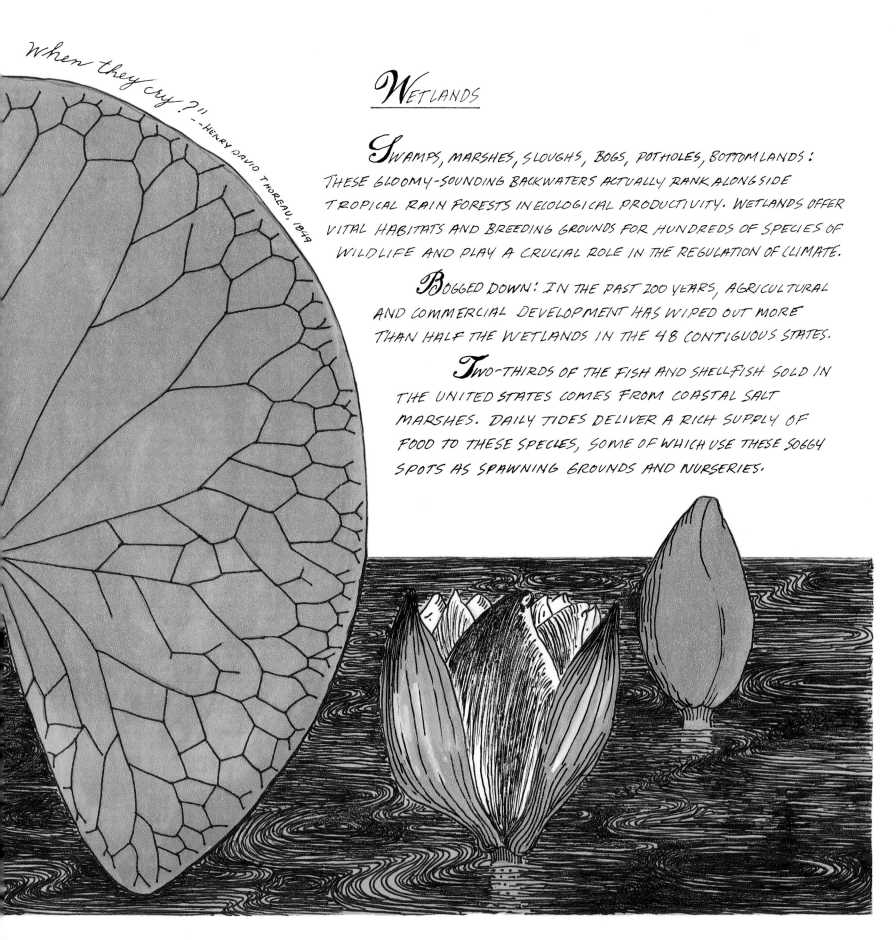

When they cry?" --HENRY DAVID THOREAU, 1849

Wetlands

Swamps, marshes, sloughs, bogs, potholes, bottomlands: these gloomy-sounding backwaters actually rank alongside tropical rain forests in ecological productivity. Wetlands offer vital habitats and breeding grounds for hundreds of species of wildlife and play a crucial role in the regulation of climate.

Bogged down: In the past 200 years, agricultural and commercial development has wiped out more than half the wetlands in the 48 contiguous states.

Two-thirds of the fish and shellfish sold in the United States comes from coastal salt marshes. Daily tides deliver a rich supply of food to these species, some of which use these soggy spots as spawning grounds and nurseries.

WHITING EGG

NUDIBRANCH EGG MASS

DOG WELK EGG CAPSULES

SQUID EGG CHAMBER

Freedom of Choice

The only hard and fast rule of mating Down Under is: Go for it. Do whatever works: ladies' choice, harems, hermaphrodites, group sex, transsexuals, couples, broadcast, merging ----

The regalia of reproduction includes fairly standard equipment. Male glands produce sperm, females produce eggs; hermaphrodites produce both. For external fertilization, marine animals or fish get together and expel a lot of eggs and sperm in the same general vicinity. One of the partners may then tend the eggs carefully until they hatch, or both may abandon their potential progeny. In the case of internal fertilization, the eggs usually stay inside the female and the male has some sort of appendage adapted for the transfer of sperm. Some of these species have live births.

A mature spawning starfish can produce more than a million eggs. If all its offspring survived and reproduced for fifteen generations, they would overrun the entire planet.

BLENNY EGG

SKATE EGG CASE

PILCHARD EGG

PORT JACKSON SHARK EGG CASE

GURNARD
EGG

OCTOPUS EGG

CHIMAERA
EGG CASE

SNAIL EGG
CAPSULE

NAUTILUS EGG
CAPSULE

$\mathcal{M}$ASS SPAWNING IN THE CORAL BELT, BETWEEN THE LATITUDES OF 30 DEGREES NORTH AND SOUTH, OCCURS SEASONALLY. CORAL POLYPS SIMULTANEOUSLY RELEASE AN EXPLOSION OF SPECTACULAR PINK SPERM AND EGGS THAT UNITE IN THE FOAMING SEA. THE CORAL LARVAE DRIFT ON THE OCEAN CURRENT, SOMETIMES FOR WEEKS, BEFORE THE SURVIVORS SETTLE ONTO ROCKS OR DEAD CORALHEADS, SECURING THEMSELVES BY SECRETING A CALCIUM COMPOUND. THESE PIONEERS EVENTUALLY CREATE A COLONY BY BUDDING OFF TO FORM SIBLINGS.

$\mathcal{S}$OME FEMALE CRABS AND LOBSTERS CAN MATE ONLY AFTER MOLTING, PLACING THEM AT THE MERCY OF THE MALE, WHO CAN CHOOSE TO EITHER FERTILIZE THEM OR EAT THEM.

$\mathcal{T}$HE AMERICAN GAFF-TOPSAIL CATFISH (SO NAMED BECAUSE OF ITS DORSAL FIN RIGGING), THE SPINY SEA CATFISH AND THE CARDINALFISH ARE ALL MOUTHBREEDERS. AFTER FERTILIZATION THE MALE TAKES ABOUT 50 OF THE 1/4-INCH EGGS INTO HIS MOUTH, WHERE THEY DEVELOP, LIVING OFF THEIR OWN YOLKS, WHILE HE FASTS UNTIL THEY HATCH.

DRAGONET
EGG

GOBY
EGG

STICKLEBACK
EGG

WEEVER
EGG

DOGFISH EMBRYO

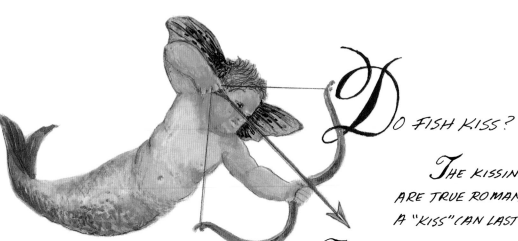

$\mathcal{D}$O FISH KISS?

$\mathcal{T}$HE KISSING GOURAMI, A SPECIES OF LABYRINTH FISH, ARE TRUE ROMANTICS KNOWN FOR THEIR PASSIONATE KISSING. A "KISS" CAN LAST AS LONG AS 25 MINUTES.

$\mathcal{F}$ISH SOMETIMES FIND IT DIFFICULT TO DETERMINE IF ANOTHER MEMBER OF THEIR OWN SPECIES IS MALE OR FEMALE, BUT WHEN MALES BEGIN THEIR RITUALISTIC DISPLAYS THEY REVEAL THEIR GENDER IN DUE COURSE. A FISH THAT IS UNWILLING TO FIGHT RAISES THE WHITE FLAG BY HUGGING HIS FINS CLOSE TO HIS BODY. IF FISH DO DUEL, THE WEAKER WILL EVENTUALLY SIGNAL ITS SUBMISSION BY PRESENTING HIS BELLY, THE MOST VULNERABLE PART OF HIS BODY. THE WINNER ACKNOWLEDGES HIS VICTORY BY CEASING HIS ATTACK.

Kissing Gourami

A FEMALE WILL SHOW SHE'S IN THE MOOD WITH GRACEFUL, SINUOUS SWIMMING. COAXING HER MATE LIKE AN EXPERIENCED COURTESAN, THE FEMALE PIPEFISH TWINES HER BODY AROUND HIM. TOGETHER THEY RISE TO THE WATER'S SURFACE, WHERE THEY RELEASE THEIR EGGS AND THEIR MILT, ALSO KNOWN AS SPERM.

FISH COURTSHIP HAS MUCH IN COMMON WITH THE ELIZABETHAN BALL, INCLUDING THE MUSIC. RIVAL MALES SWIM SIDE-BY-SIDE AND BEAT THEIR TAILS IN THE WATER.

IN ONE BREED OF CHARACIN, FOUND IN THE AMAZON JUNGLE, THE LOVERS LOCK FINS AND LEAP OUT OF THE WATER TOGETHER. THE FEMALE DEPOSITS HER EGGS ON A LEAF OR BRANCH OVERHANGING THE BANKS OF A RIVER. TO KEEP THE EGGS FROM DRYING OUT DURING THEIR 3-DAY INCUBATION PERIOD, THE MALE SPLASHES THEM WITH HIS TAIL.

Be it Ever so Humble

Beyond the architectural splendor of the undersea reef cities, in the bucolic coziness of rivers, lakes, and ponds, many fish follow an instinct for family values and build, of all things, nests.

Shoals, or schools, of stickleback fishes migrate from deeper coastal waters to shallow, preferably sandy, sites as the spawning season approaches. Males resplendent in their nuptial garb wear ruby collars and cummerbunds as they excavate shallow pits with their fins, and deposit in them strands of algae, aquatic leaves, and roots. Swimming solemnly back and forth over the loose pile, they secrete a sticky substance from their kidneys to glue the mass together. Next, they create a tunnel by boring a hole in each end of their creation; then they swim inside to push up the ceiling. The proud stickleback entices the female to come inside, where she lays her eggs before leaving by the back door. After fertilizing the eggs, the doting father cares for them until they hatch, adjusting the nest's openings for ventilation and repairing it as necessary.

Male lip-fish of the Mediterranean build cup-shaped nests that resemble those of the terrestrial blackbird.

Freshwater female African cichlids excavate pits for their nests.

Sea Stickleback Nest on Seaweed

Jaw fish and tile fish off the coast of Southeast Asia are master stone and tile masons. With their massive jaws, they dredge out wells and then painstakingly line them with shells and pebbles fitted artfully together.

Male labyrinth and paradise fish from the remote Asian tropics and sub-tropics create nests of long lasting air bubbles at the water's surface. Eggs contributed by the female contain a lighter-than-water blob of oil that lets them rise and nestle under the bubble dome.

French sand gobies shop around for an empty half-shell from a bivalve mollusk. When they find the home of their dreams, they excavate a basement underneath and pile sand on top of the shell, leaving only its rim visible. A narrow access channel admits the female, who deposits her eggs on the ceiling of the nest.

Ocellated Sand Goby

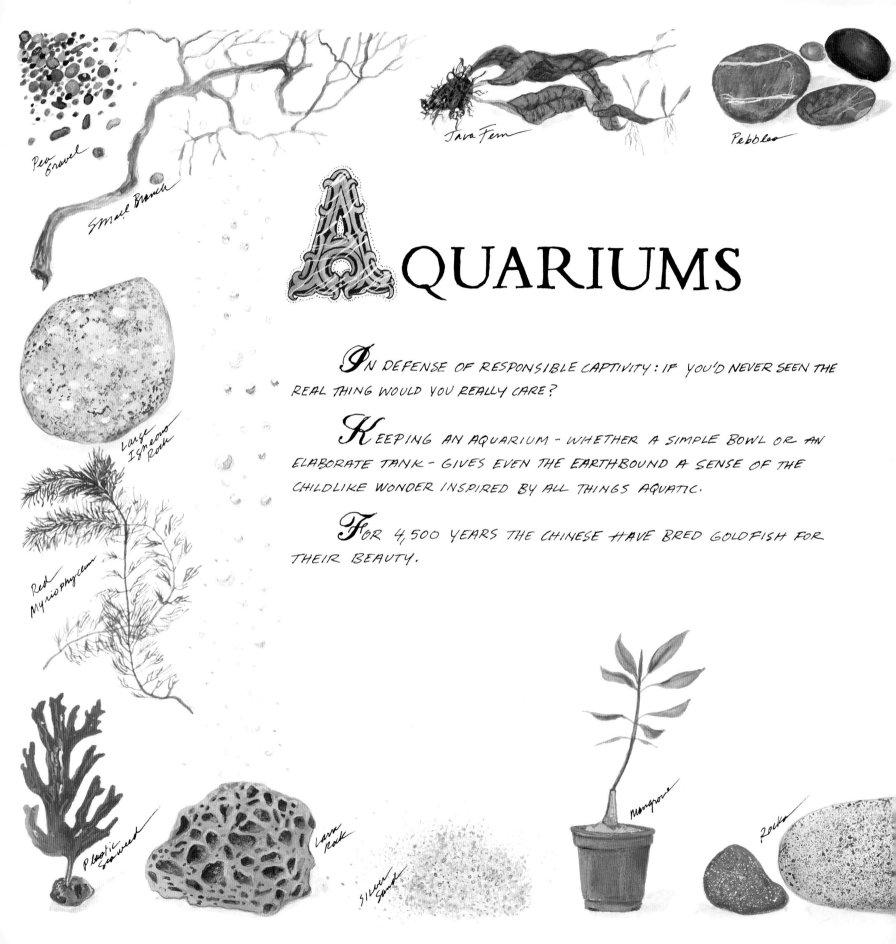

AQUARIUMS

In defense of responsible captivity: if you'd never seen the real thing would you really care?

Keeping an aquarium - whether a simple bowl or an elaborate tank - gives even the earthbound a sense of the childlike wonder inspired by all things aquatic.

For 4,500 years the Chinese have bred goldfish for their beauty.

Pea Gravel

Small Branch

Java Fern

Pebbles

Large Igneous Rock

Red Myriophyllum

Plastic Seaweed

Lava Rock

Silver Sand

Mangrove

Rocks

The Assyrians kept fish in ponds 4,000 years ago and expressed their admiration for the animals by depicting them on coins.

The first modern public aquariums were built in the early 19th century. In 1846, one Mrs. Thynne of England made the first attempt to keep marine fish alive and to maintain healthy water conditions for them. Six years later, the first large-scale public aquarium opened in London.

The road to conservation and preservation begins with study and understanding. For the armchair diver or budding biologist, a visit to the aquarium offers a window on an endlessly fascinating world.

Aquariums, like zoos, serve as gene banks where marine biologists can work to preserve endangered species.

More than Vanity

Survival in the sea requires strict economy: every act and feature of every life form must serve a purpose. If the riot of colors found in the deep offered no advantage, then natural selection or random genetic drift would erase the bold hues.

Herbivores that frequent algae-filled water have adopted the algal colors as camouflage. Other animals, such as anemones, or corals, who need to broadcast a visual message have evolved colors that contrast with the monotone algae.

Cells called chromatophores produce brown, black, yellow, orange and red pigments in the skin of fish, while iridocytes generate the iridescent colors, especially bright greens and blues. With exquisite neuromuscular control, some fish can perform resplendent color shifts of varying speeds and intensities.

Conspicuous color can signal availability for mating; it also helps define territorial boundaries and confuse predators.

Killifish

Gamora hemichrysos

Epalzeorhynchus kallopterus

Caris angulata

Guppy

Red-Nosed Tetra

caris gaimardi

Brilliantly colored fishes can easily hide from their enemies in the reefs they inhabit. Quick and agile, they have ample ecological justification for their ostentatious appearance.

Pearl Danio

Guppy

Guppy

Brachydanio frankei

Guppy

Hasemania marginata

Guppy

Guppy

Guppy

Guppy

Swordtail

Dwarf Gourami

Borelli's Dwarf Cichlid

Bumblebee Fish

Flame Fish

Pomacentrus melanochir

Many vivid species defy the fashions of the camouflage crowd and sport electrifying colors and bold patterns that seem to have no simple explanation.

CARP & GOLDFISH

An aquatic yin-yang, the warrior carp also represents love.

Koi, or Japanese carp, are said to have been first bred in northern Japan on the island of Honshu during the Hei-an period (794-1184 A.D.). They represent masculinity and strength.

While koi are bred for their spectacular white, gold, red and mixed coloration, goldfish are bred for their frilly fins and varied body shapes.

The dime store goldfish makes an unassuming household pet, but it is, in fact, a noble creature of ancient pedigree.

WHAT FIRST DREW THE CHINESE TO CHIN-YI, OR GOLDFISH? PERHAPS IT WAS THEIR LUCKY RED COLORING, THEIR PEACEFUL NATURE, AND THEIR DEMURE HABITS. WHATEVER THE SOURCE OF THE ATTRACTION, IT HAS INSPIRED THEM TO CULTIVATE DOMESTICATED GOLDFISH FOR THOUSANDS OF YEARS.

IS THE CARP A GROUCH? OUR LANGUAGE SEEMS TO SUGGEST AS MUCH: TO CARP IS TO RAISE UNNECESSARY OR TRIVIAL OBJECTIONS; TO CARP AT IS TO SCOLD OR FIND FAULT CONSTANTLY; A CARP IS A COMPLAINT AND A CARPER THE PERSON WHO MAKES IT. POOR, MALIGNED CARP!

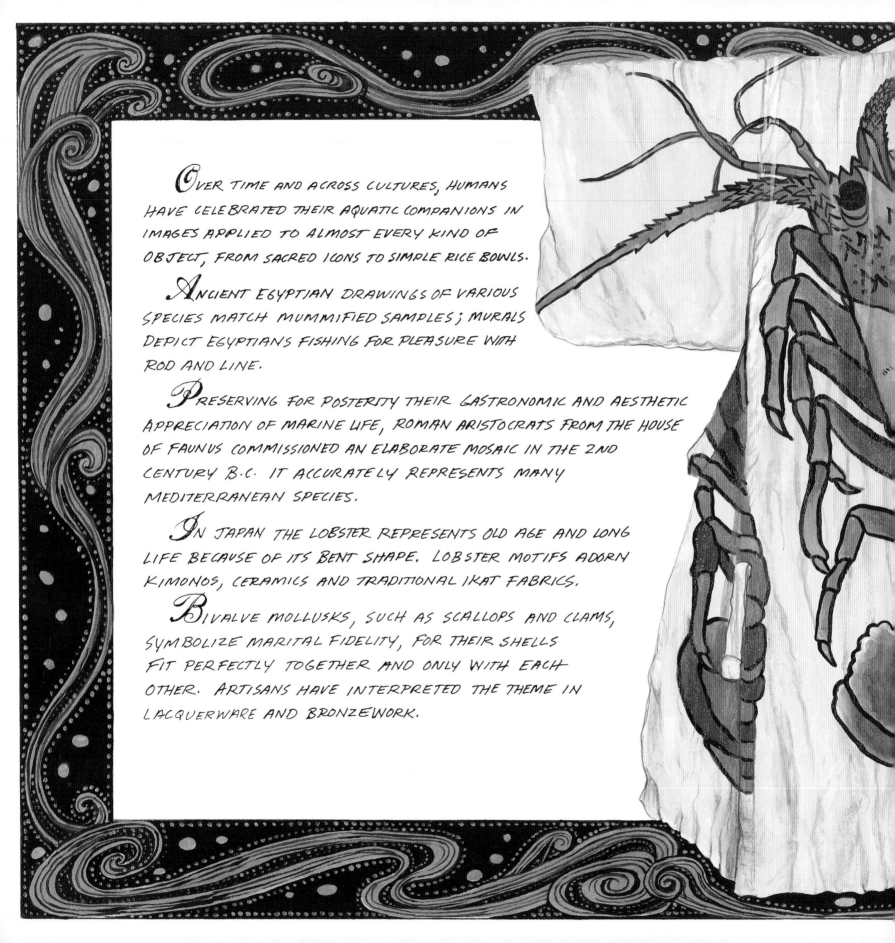

Over time and across cultures, humans have celebrated their aquatic companions in images applied to almost every kind of object, from sacred icons to simple rice bowls.

Ancient Egyptian drawings of various species match mummified samples; murals depict Egyptians fishing for pleasure with rod and line.

Preserving for posterity their gastronomic and aesthetic appreciation of marine life, Roman aristocrats from the house of Faunus commissioned an elaborate mosaic in the 2nd century B.C. It accurately represents many Mediterranean species.

In Japan the lobster represents old age and long life because of its bent shape. Lobster motifs adorn kimonos, ceramics and traditional ikat fabrics.

Bivalve mollusks, such as scallops and clams, symbolize marital fidelity, for their shells fit perfectly together and only with each other. Artisans have interpreted the theme in lacquerware and bronzework.

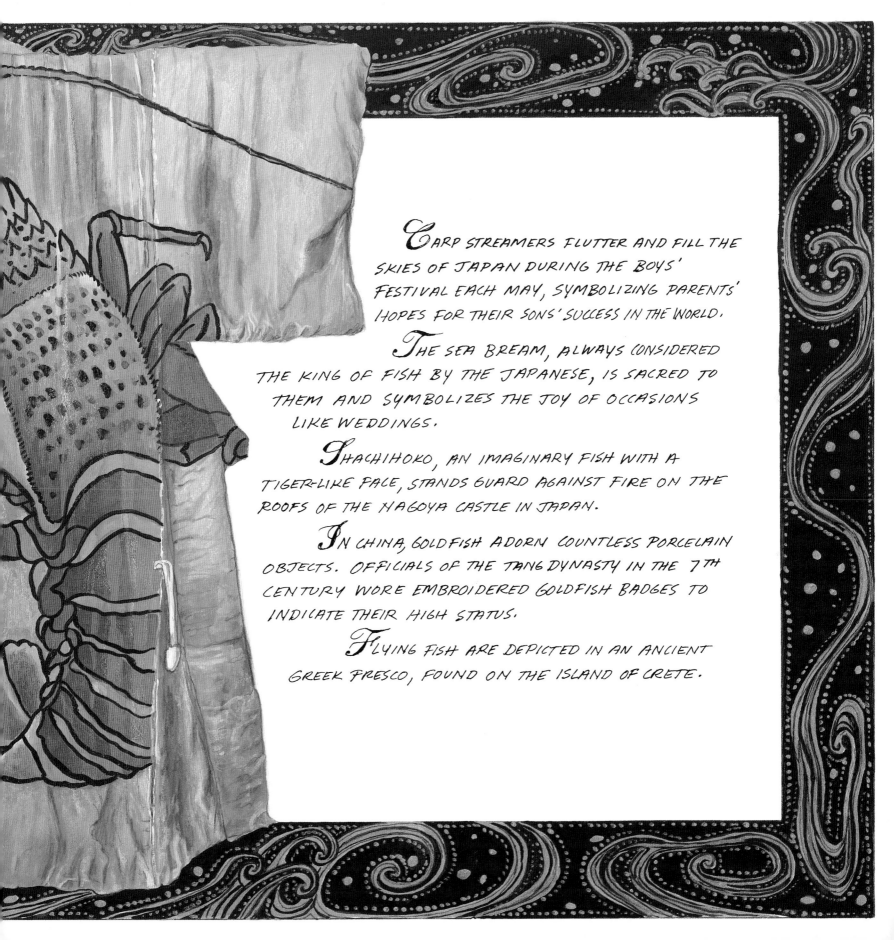

Carp streamers flutter and fill the skies of Japan during the Boys' Festival each May, symbolizing parents' hopes for their sons' success in the world.

The sea bream, always considered the king of fish by the Japanese, is sacred to them and symbolizes the joy of occasions like weddings.

Shachihoko, an imaginary fish with a tiger-like face, stands guard against fire on the roofs of the Nagoya Castle in Japan.

In China, goldfish adorn countless porcelain objects. Officials of the Tang Dynasty in the 7th century wore embroidered goldfish badges to indicate their high status.

Flying fish are depicted in an ancient Greek fresco, found on the island of Crete.

Lobsters & Crayfish

Some Like it Hot

RED AND WHITE SPECIES OF CRAYFISH HAVE ADAPTED WELL TO THE WATERS OF THE BAYOU COUNTRY OF LOUISIANA, AND LOUSIANIANS HAVE ADAPTED AS WELL TO THE SWEET TENDERNESS OF CRAWDADDY MEAT. THE ANIMALS ARE A STAPLE OF SPICY CAJUN COOKING.

EUROPEAN LOBSTERS WHO EVADE BEING CAUGHT FOR FOOD CAN REACH THE VENERABLE AGE OF 50 TO 100 YEARS AND GROW TO THREE FEET IN LENGTH.

LOBSTERMEN IN THE UNITED STATES HAUL IN 50 MILLION POUNDS OF AMERICAN LOBSTER EACH YEAR. AMERICANS ANNUALLY IMPORT ANOTHER 30 MILLION POUNDS OF THE DELICACY FROM CANADA.

PRISONERS IN 19TH-CENTURY MAINE FEASTED ON LOBSTER, FOR LAW-ABIDING CITIZENS CONSIDERED THE CREATURES "TRASH FISH" FIT ONLY FOR ANIMALS AND CONVICTS.

PEOPLE LIVING AROUND THE MEDITERRANEAN SEA, ONE OF THE WORLD'S RICHEST MARINE ENVIRONMENTS, RELISH SEAFOOD, PARTICULARLY SHELLFISH.

Riding to Health

on FISH and SEA FOOD

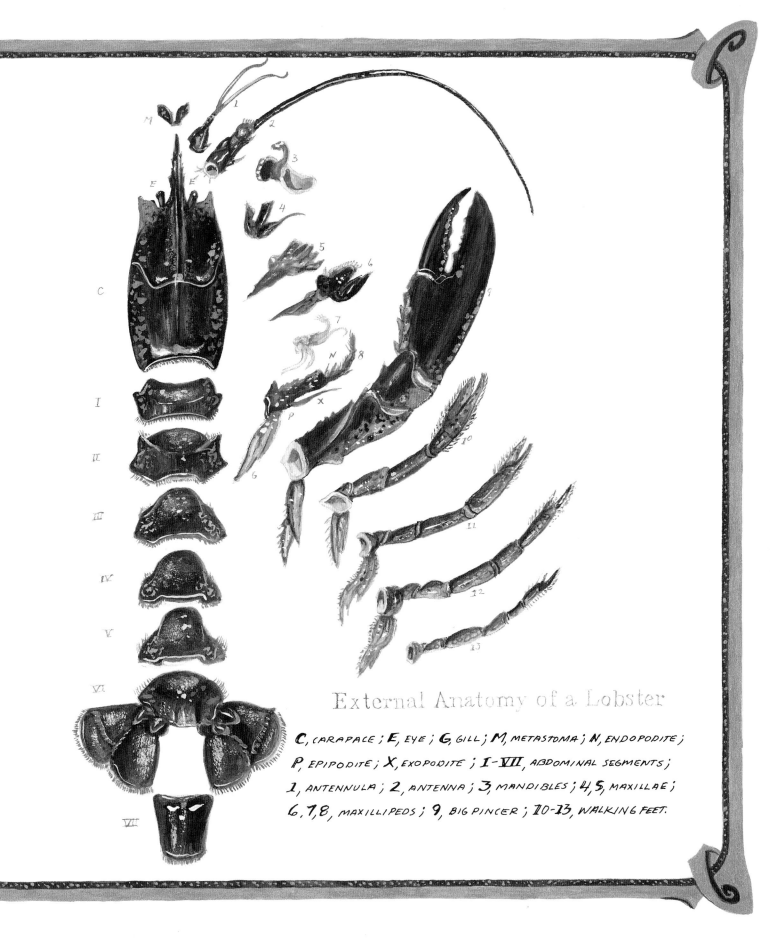

External Anatomy of a Lobster

C, CARAPACE ; E, EYE ; G, GILL ; M, METASTOMA ; N, ENDOPODITE ;
P, EPIPODITE ; X, EXOPODITE ; I–VII, ABDOMINAL SEGMENTS ;
1, ANTENNULA ; 2, ANTENNA ; 3, MANDIBLES ; 4, 5, MAXILLAE ;
6, 7, 8, MAXILLIPEDS ; 9, BIG PINCER ; 10–13, WALKING FEET.

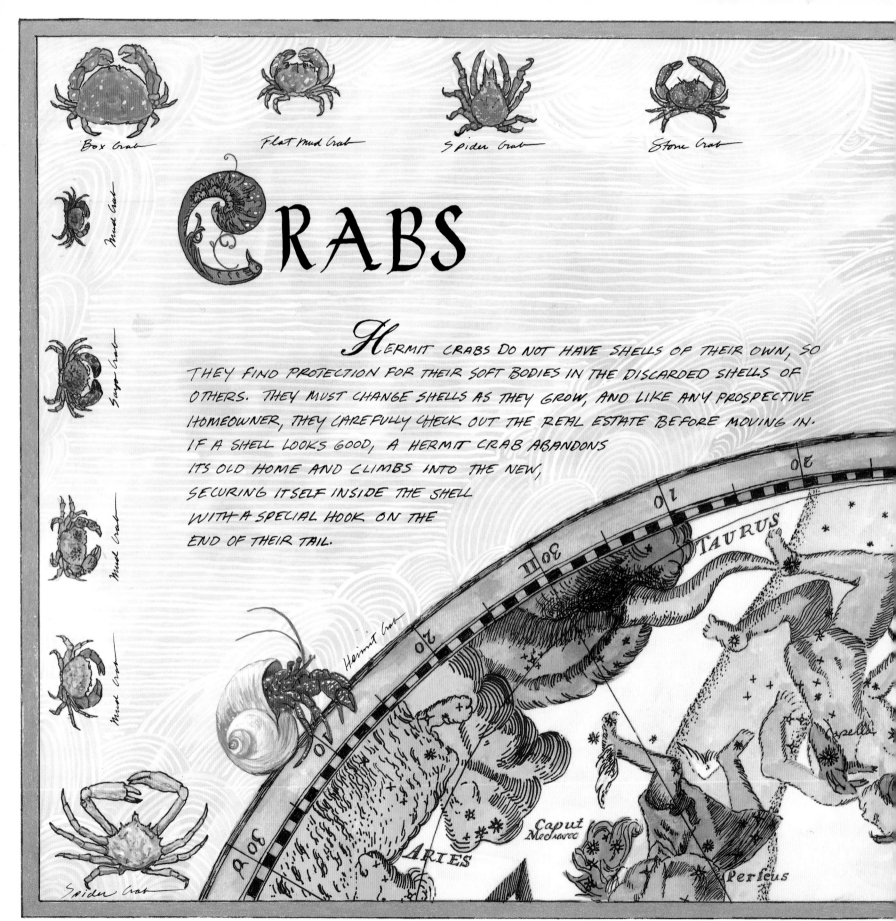

CRABS

HERMIT CRABS DO NOT HAVE SHELLS OF THEIR OWN, SO THEY FIND PROTECTION FOR THEIR SOFT BODIES IN THE DISCARDED SHELLS OF OTHERS. THEY MUST CHANGE SHELLS AS THEY GROW, AND LIKE ANY PROSPECTIVE HOMEOWNER, THEY CAREFULLY CHECK OUT THE REAL ESTATE BEFORE MOVING IN. IF A SHELL LOOKS GOOD, A HERMIT CRAB ABANDONS ITS OLD HOME AND CLIMBS INTO THE NEW, SECURING ITSELF INSIDE THE SHELL WITH A SPECIAL HOOK ON THE END OF THEIR TAIL.

Box Crab

Flat Mud Crab

Spider Crab

Stone Crab

Mud Crab

Surge Crab

Mud Crab

Mud Crab

Spider Crab

Hermit Crab

TAURUS

Caput Medusae

ARIES

Perseus

Capella

Fiddler Crab

Common Spider Crab

parchment Worm Crab

Toad Crab

Wooly Crab

Mud Crab

Oyster Crab

Blue Swimming Crab

Calico Crab

The Crab That Ate Tokyo

The largest of all crustaceans is a monster: the hulking Japanese spider crab, found in the North Pacific, spans 12 feet with its enormous claws outstretched. Its carapace can measure 18 inches across—inspiration for many Japanese horror flicks.

The robber or coconut crab climbs trees on the beach in search of coconuts, which it cracks in half with its claws. It lives in half of the coconut shell.

Ancient astronomers saw a crab-like pattern of stars in the northern sky and named the constellation Cancer, the Latin word for crab. The sun passes through the fourth sign of the zodiac between June 21 and July 22.

Today astrologers tend to stress the maternal aspects of this sign, which is ruled by the great mother, the moon. Originally, though, seers emphasized the crab's hard shell, as Cancerians are reputed to be a bit thick-skinned.

GEMINI

CANCER

Magnitudinestellarum

HRIMP & KRILL

Krill

Traveling in swarms of millions, krill can quite literally be scared out of their skins by attacking predators. They instantaneously molt and flee en masse, leaving behind a ghostly school of exoskeletons as a decoy.

A staple food for threatened Antarctic wildlife such as the baleen whale, the thumb-length krill now face a new predator: humankind. The ocean's richest source of protein, krill are being processed into feed for livestock and farmed fish. Alarmed marine biologists fear the vast harvests might threaten the species and break a vital link in the food chain.

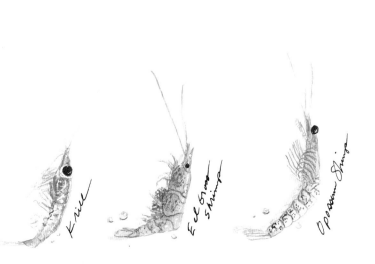

Shrimp

Chefs may disagree, but to a zoologist the terms prawn and shrimp are often interchangeable. Australian prawns grow as large as Maine lobsters, while giant river prawns reach a foot or more in length.

These crustaceans wear a variety of colors—green, white, brown, yellow, banana, and pink—for which they are named. And pass it on—pink shrimp are the reason why flamingos who feast on them are pink.

Pistol shrimp are the sharpshooters of the sea. These shrimpy little banditos measure only two inches long, but they pack a powerful wallop. When a fish wanders by, the pistol shrimp ambushes it with its right claw, which is equipped with a matching peg and hole. The shrimp releases the striker from the hole in its claw to create a shock wave that stuns the fish momentarily, then it moves in for the kill.

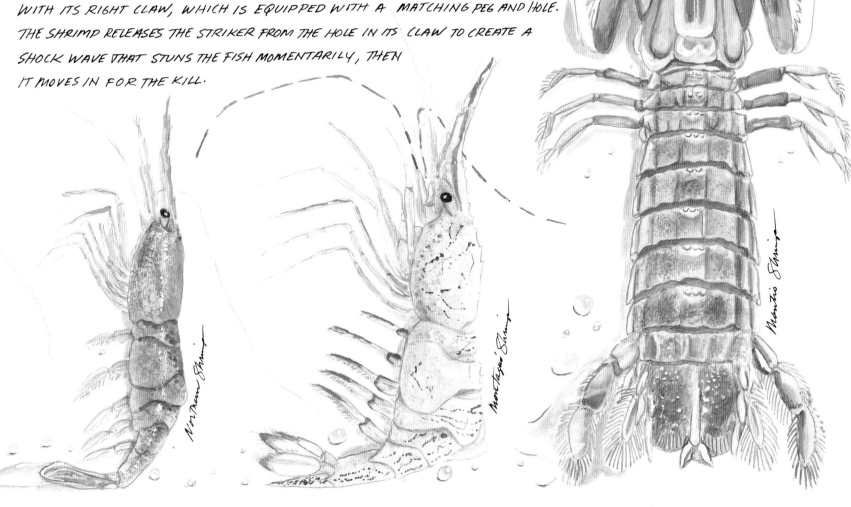

Northern Shrimp

Montague Shrimp

Mantis Shrimp

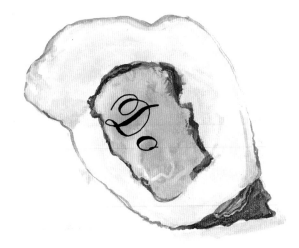

TODAY IN MODERN IRELAND, APPLYING THE TENCH FISH -- KNOWN AS "THE PHYSICIAN OF FISHES" -- TO THE SOLES OF THE FEET IS THE THING TO DO FOR JAUNDICE.

FOR PREGNANT WOMEN IN JAPAN, INDIA AND WEST AFRICA, HOLDING A COWRIE SHELL IN THE HAND IS THE THING TO DO TO ENSURE A SAFE AND EASY CHILDBIRTH.

TO KEEP THE CHINESE SEA MONK, THE TERROR OF THE EASTERN SEAS, AT BAY, A RITUAL DANCE IS THE THING TO DO.

FOR WEALTHY ROMANS, KEEPING MORAY EELS AS PETS AND DECORATING THEM WITH JEWELRY WAS THE THING TO DO. FEEDING THEM DISOBEDIENT OR UNWANTED SLAVES WAS ALSO THE THING TO DO.

WEARING COSMETICS MADE OF PURPLE DYE EXTRACTED FROM MOLLUSKS WAS THE THING TO DO FOR THE LADIES OF ANCIENT ROME. WHITENING AND SOFTENING THE SKIN WITH A FACE PACK OF SNAIL POWDER AND BEAN MEAL WAS ALSO THE THING TO DO.

IN NINETEENTH CENTURY ENGLAND, EATING RARE AND EXPENSIVE OYSTERS WAS THE THING TO DO AMONG THE UPPER CLASSES.

TRADITIONAL FISH REMEDIES THAT WERE ONCE THE THING TO DO: AN ECZEMA SALVE MADE FROM SNAILS; A SCAR-FADER MADE OF COCKLE BROTH; A COUGH SYRUP MADE OF SNAIL MUCILAGE.

The Oyster Lover

Taboo

ANTHROPOLOGIST MARGARET MEAD REPORTED THAT PRESENTING A SOUTH SEAS CHIEF WITH A BRIGHTLY COLORED FISH WAS TABOO UNTIL WATER WAS POURED OVER IT.

FOR POLYNESIANS WHO HAD A PERSONAL SHARK OR EEL TOTEM, EATING THESE CREATURES WAS TABOO.

AMONG THE ANCIENT JEWS, AND EVEN TODAY, EATING SHELLFISH WAS TABOO, EXCEPT BY SPECIAL EDICT.

FOR THE SERBIANS, THE CONSUMPTION OF FISH BY PREGNANT WOMEN IS TABOO.

FOR THE TASMANIAN ABORIGINALS, EATING FISH WITH SCALES WAS TABOO.

FOR THE BANTUS, EATING FISH AT ALL IS TABOO.

"A lake is the landscape's most beautiful and expressive feature. It is earth's eye: looking into which the beholder measures the depth of his own nature."

HENRY DAVID THOREAU, <u>WALDEN</u>, 1854

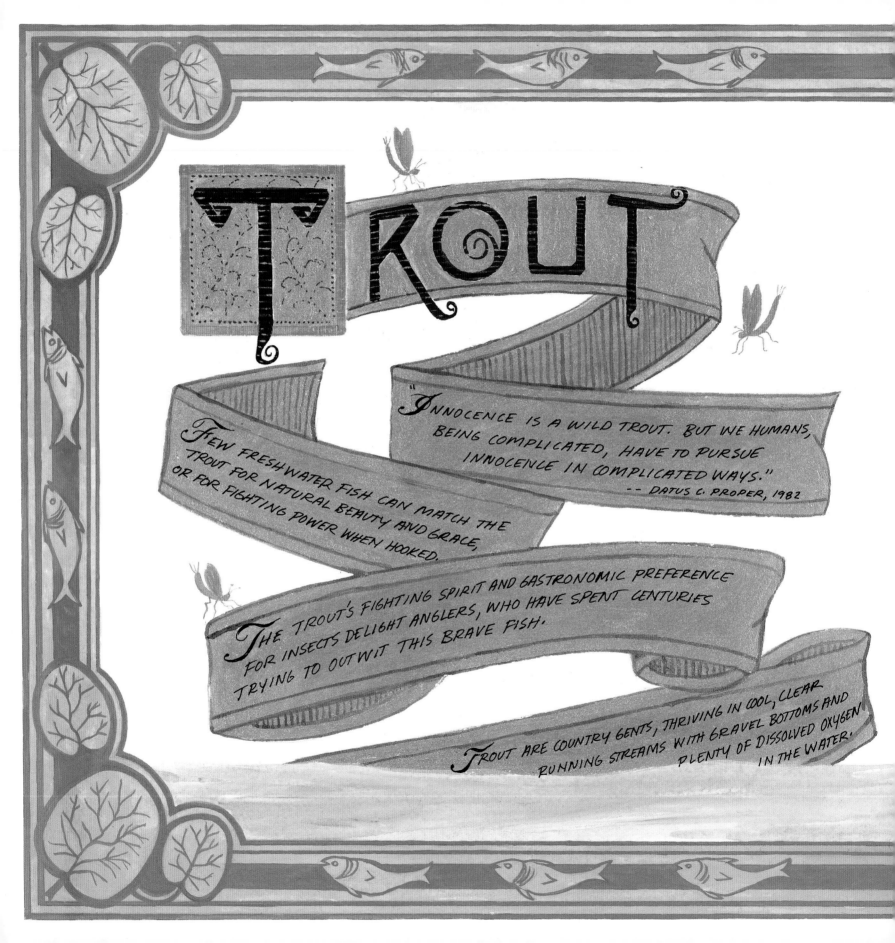

TROUT

"INNOCENCE IS A WILD TROUT. BUT WE HUMANS, BEING COMPLICATED, HAVE TO PURSUE INNOCENCE IN COMPLICATED WAYS."
-- DATUS C. PROPER, 1982

FEW FRESHWATER FISH CAN MATCH THE TROUT FOR NATURAL BEAUTY AND GRACE, OR FOR FIGHTING POWER WHEN HOOKED.

THE TROUT'S FIGHTING SPIRIT AND GASTRONOMIC PREFERENCE FOR INSECTS DELIGHT ANGLERS, WHO HAVE SPENT CENTURIES TRYING TO OUTWIT THIS BRAVE FISH.

TROUT ARE COUNTRY GENTS, THRIVING IN COOL, CLEAR RUNNING STREAMS WITH GRAVEL BOTTOMS AND PLENTY OF DISSOLVED OXYGEN IN THE WATER.

PERCIFORMS MAKE UP THE LARGEST ORDER OF FISH, WITH OVER 150 FAMILIES AND 8,000 SPECIES. HERRING, PERCH, BASS, COD AND MULLET ARE THE MOST FAMILIAR OF THESE NUMEROUS FISH.

COME ALONG AND FOLLOW ME
TO THE BOTTOM OF THE SEA
WE WILL JOIN THE JAMBOREE
AT THE CODFISH BALL.
   LOBSTERS DANCING IN A ROW
SHUFFLE OFF TO BUFFALO
JELLYFISH SWAY TO AND FRO
AT THE CODFISH BALL.
   FIN AND HADDIE LEAD THE EELS
THROUGH AN IRISH REEL
THE CATFISH IS A DANCING MAN
BUT HE CAN'T CAN-CAN
LIKE THE SARDINE CAN.
   TUNAS TRUCKIN' LEFT AND RIGHT
MINNIE'S MOOCHIN' THROUGH THE NIGHT
THERE WON'T BE A HOOK IN SIGHT
AT THE CODFISH BALL.

   -- "AT THE CODFISH BALL," SIDNEY MITCHELL
AND LEW POLLACK

Most Confusing

MOST PICKLED, CANNED, SALTED, AND SMOKED SARDINES ARE, IN FACT, SMALL HERRINGS SOLD UNDER THAT NAME. SARDINES EARN THE APPELLATION "FATS" WHEN THEY REACH 10 INCHES IN LENGTH, BECAUSE AT THAT SIZE THEY HAVE ENOUGH FAT IN THEIR BODIES TO MAKE THEM A VALUABLE SOURCE OF OIL.

Length 45MM.

50MM

JUN. 1

60MM.

70MM.

JULY

80MM.

AUG. 1

90MM.

Young Herring
SHOWING RATE OF GROWTH DURING FIRST YEAR OF LIFE, ACTUAL SIZE. BORN IN DECEMBER TO JANUARY.

Red Mullet

Atlantic Cod

Respect Your Elders

THE GIANT SEA BASS RULES THE TOP OF THE FOOD CHAIN AT THE BOTTOM OF THE SEA; OTHER FISH LIVE ONLY BY ITS LEAVE.

A 770-POUND BASS MAY LIVE MORE THAN A CENTURY IF DISEASE OR ACCIDENT DOES NOT KILL IT.

Catch of the Day

Corals busily reach into the food stream with their tentacles, while butterfly fish, starfish, crabs, and a myriad of other browsers prey upon them. Carnivorous anemones and jellyfish, meanwhile, drag stunned fish toward their mouths with their tentacles.

Sponges and mollusks filter a steady current of water through their bodies, straining out nourishment and prey. This dining system is so efficient that some sponges have grown large enough to fit two human divers inside.

Sand plough snails drill holes through the shells of oysters and other mollusks by means of file-like tooth ribbons, poking their snout into the hole to devour the catch of the day.

The lizard fish, like a Buddha, sits motionless, waiting as its target moves nearer. Then in a single explosive movement it ambushes and gulps down its prey.

Butterfly Fish

Royal Gramma

Purple Sea-Star

Lizard Fish

Fiddler Crab

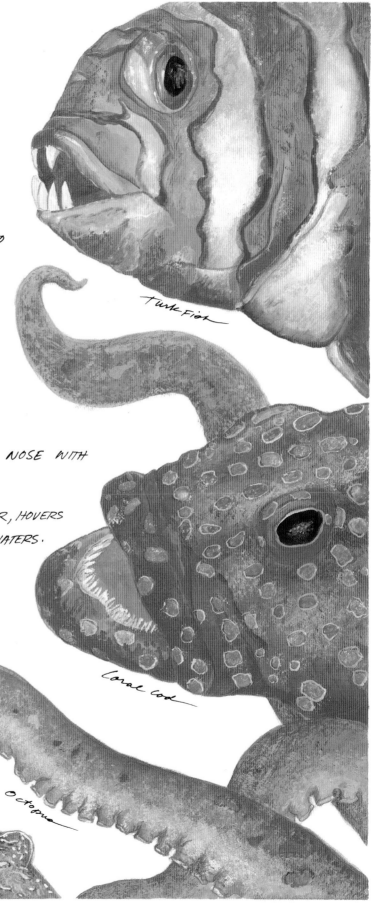

Lobsters, shrimps, and crabs cruise the coral looking to pick up other crustaceans. But a dinner date with such a mate always ends badly, with the predator crushing its prey in pincers and claws, then grinding it to a pulp with powerful jaws. Lobsters even have a set of teeth inside their stomach.

Scavengers like the sea urchin consume an extremely rich delicacy: detritus, the scummy ooze of plant and animal bits that have decomposed and settled onto rocks, sand, and mud flats. Detritus also supports the teeming life forms of the abyss and the ocean floor.

The grazing butterfly fish has developed a long nose with which it reaches into small crevices for tasty treats.

The royal gramma, always ready to dive for cover, hovers near its shelter while it snaps bits of food from passing waters.

The stocky piranha, equipped with razor-sharp interlocking teeth, hunts in packs. These bloody feeding frenzies can strip a victim down to a skeleton in a matter of minutes.

Tusk Fish

Coral Cod

Cuttlefish

Octopus

Senses and Traits

The familiar horizontal stripe that runs the length of a fish's body is a special sensing organ that helps it, among other things, to feel vibrations.

Spread over the bodies of starfish and other marine invertebrates, and located in the tentacles of octopi, receptor cells respond to touch. In much the same way, sea creatures perceive chemicals in the water by smell and taste.

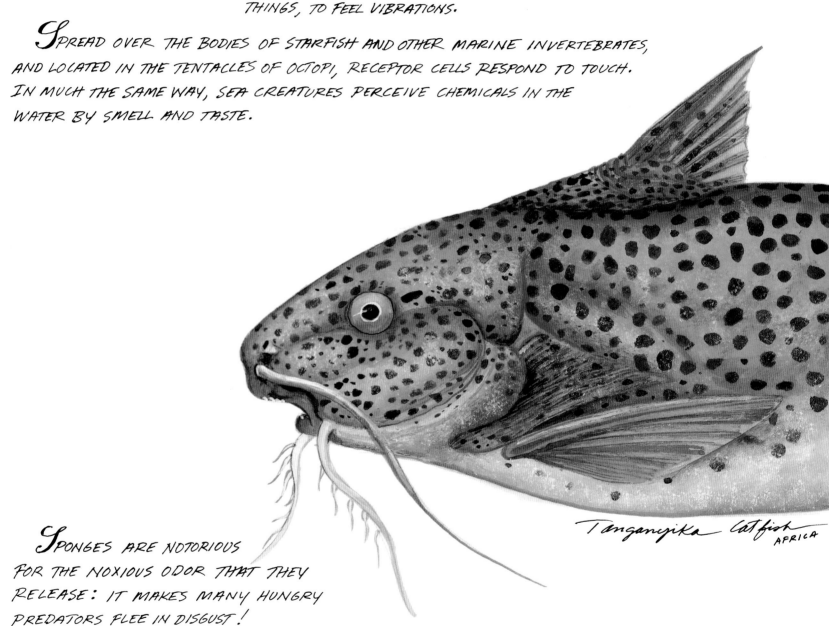

Tanganyika Catfish
AFRICA

Sponges are notorious for the noxious odor that they release: it makes many hungry predators flee in disgust!

Herring & others

Historic Herrings

The Battle of the Herrings took place in 1429, when Sir John Falstaff of England routed French forces who tried to blockade his delivery of herrings to the Duke of Suffolk, who was besieging Orleans. In the 15th century, the Dutch and the English squabbled over herring-fishing rights, as the members of the European Economic Community continue to do to this day.

The Original Red Herring

In Shakespeare's Antony and Cleopatra, Cleopatra teases Anthony when he boasts of his angling skills. The Egyptian queen hires a diver to fasten a withered red herring to her lover's hook and jerk the line. When Anthony hauls in the sorry fish Cleopatra laughs, but the clever fisherman finds a way out: he announces he has hooked the oldest fish ever caught with a fishing pole.

No Exaggeration

Fishermen report running into "mountains" of herring and cod that are capable of capsizing small boats. These closely packed masses of spawning fish swim in layers, sometimes covering one square mile of water.

Atlantic Cod

"IN OUR FAMILY, THERE WAS NO CLEAR LINE BETWEEN RELIGION AND FLY FISHING. WE LIVED AT THE JUNCTION OF GREAT TROUT RIVERS IN WESTERN MONTANA, AND OUR FATHER WAS A PRESBYTERIAN MINISTER AND A FLY FISHERMAN WHO TAUGHT OTHERS. HE TOLD US ABOUT CHRIST'S DISCIPLES BEING FISHERMEN, AND WE WERE LEFT TO ASSUME, AS MY BROTHER AND I DID, THAT ALL FIRST-CLASS FISHERMEN ON THE SEA OF GALILEE WERE FLY FISHERMEN AND THAT JOHN, THE FAVORITE, WAS A DRY-FLY FISHERMAN."

-- A RIVER RUNS THROUGH IT, NORMAN MACLEAN, 1976

"TO CAPTURE THE FISH IS NOT ALL OF THE FISHING."

-- ZANE GREY, 1919

"FISHERMEN ARE NOT UNLIKE THEIR QUARRY: THEY GO THROUGH STAGES OF EVOLUTION. INITIALLY THEY START OUT AS HONEST MEN BUT SOON ADAPT."

-- ATTRIBUTED TO CHARLES DARWIN

"ALSO, YOU MUST NOT BE GREEDY IN YOUR CATCH, SO AS TO TAKE TOO MANY FISH AT ONE TIME, WHICH YOU MAY DO UNTHINKINGLY... WHICH WILL CAUSE YOU TO DESTROY YOUR OWN SPORT AND THAT OF OTHER MEN...."

-- ATTRIBUTED TO DAME JULIANA BERNERS

"SO IF TO RAISE SOME HONEST KIDS IS YOUR FONDEST WISH, JUST LEAD 'EM TO THE WATER AND TEACH 'EM HOW TO FISH."

-- ED STONE, 1973

"I DON'T KNOW WHY I OR OTHER MEN FISH, EXCEPT THAT WE LIKE IT AND IT MAKES US THINK AND FEEL...A RIVER...HAS ITS OWN LIFE AND ITS OWN BEAUTY, AND THE CREATURES THAT IT NOURISHES ARE ALIVE AND BEAUTIFUL ALSO. PERHAPS FISHING IS, FOR ME, ONLY AN EXCUSE TO BE NEAR RIVERS...."

-- RODERICK L. HAIG-BROWN, 1944

AND PASSING ALONG THE SEA OF GALILEE, JESUS SAW SIMON AND ANDREW THE BROTHER OF SIMON CASTING A NET IN THE SEA, FOR THEY WERE FISHERMEN. AND JESUS SAID TO THEM, 'FOLLOW ME AND I WILL MAKE YOU BECOME FISHERS OF MEN."

MATTHEW 4:18-9
MARK 1:16-17

$\mathcal{T}$HE FISH'S FORMIDABLE SENSE OF SMELL SHOWS UP MOST
CHILLINGLY IN THE STALKING HABITS OF CARNIVOROUS SHARKS, WHO
CAN SENSE ONE PART BLOOD TO ONE MILLION PARTS WATER.

$\mathcal{S}$ALMON RETURNING FROM THE OPEN OCEAN TO SPAWN IN THEIR
NATAL RIVERS HONE IN ON THE SCENT OF HOME BY FOLLOWING THE
OLFACTORY CLUES IMPRINTED AT HATCHING.

$\mathcal{C}$ATFISH TOUCH AND TASTE WITH THEIR
WHISKERLIKE BARBELS.

*W*HAT'S IN A NAME?

*M*ANY FISH HAVE FANTASTIC SNOUTS THAT HAVE EARNED THEM WHIMSICAL NAMES. AMONG THEM:

*M*ARLINS ARE NAMED FOR THE POINTED IRON TOOLS THAT SEAFARERS EMPLOY WHEN MARLING, OR SPLICING ROPE.

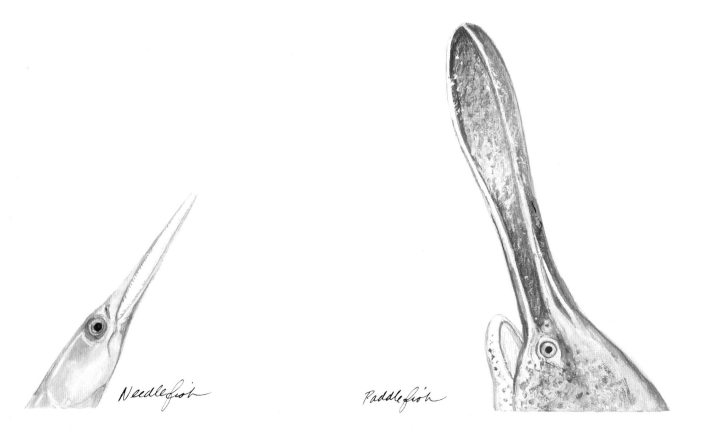

Needlefish

Paddlefish

Sawfish

Marlin

The swordfish boasts the longest snout of all -- it's 5 feet long. Touché!

Like living javelins, needlefish leap out of the water when panicked; some have pinned sailors to the sides of their boats.

Swordfish

Other evocative fish names include the Billfish, the Paddlefish and the Sawfish.

Pigfish

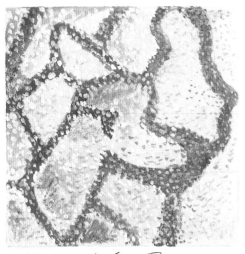

Honeycomb Cow Fish

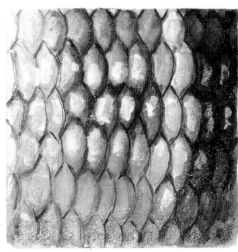

Butterfly Fish

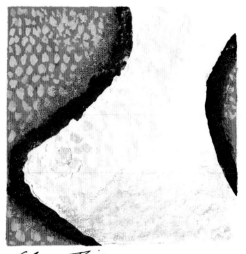

Clown Fish

Skin and Scales

MOST FISH HAVE SCALES, THIN TRANSPARENT PLATES THAT OVERLAP LIKE SHINGLES ON A ROOF AND PROTECT THE SENSITIVE SKIN BELOW. ICHTHYOLOGISTS CAN ESTIMATE THE AGE OF A FISH BY COUNTING THE GROWTH RINGS ON ITS SCALES, MUCH LIKE FORESTERS COUNT THE RINGS ON A TREE. EACH SPECIES HAS AN UNVARYING NUMBER OF ROWS OF SCALES, MAKING THE TASK OF IDENTIFICATION EASIER.

FOUR MAIN TYPES OF SCALES COVER THE FISH OF THE RIVERS AND SEAS: SMOOTH, CYCLOID SCALES SPROUT ON TRUE BONY FISH SUCH AS CARP. SOME OF THESE CRITTERS — BASS, FOR INSTANCE — ALSO CARRY CTENOID SCALES THAT HAVE TINY TEETH ALONG THEIR EDGES. GANOID SCALES, SHINY, HARD AND DIAMOND-SHAPED, CHARACTERIZE PRIMITIVE BONY FISH, THE GAR AMONG THEM. MANY CARTILAGINOUS FISH, SUCH AS THE SHARK, WEAR THORNY PLACOID SCALES.

FOR CENTURIES, PEOPLE HAVE APPRECIATED THE SANDPAPER ROUGHNESS OF RAY AND SHARK SKIN, USING IT AS A NON-SLIP SWORD GRIP. WHITE SETTLERS IN NORTH AMERICA COVERED THEIR PLOUGHS WITH THE CHAIN-MAIL ARMOUR OF GARFISH SKIN.

Coral Trout

Royal Gramma

Scrolled File Fish

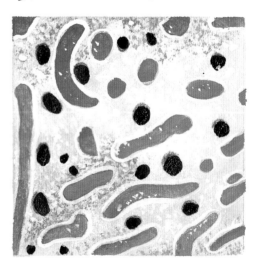

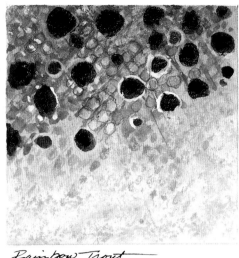

Rainbow Trout

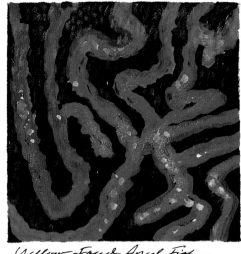

Yellow-Faced Angel Fish

Shark

Porous skin helps fish maintain the right osmotic balance between their tissue and the surrounding water. Because they can keep their internal salinity within tolerable limits, they avoid dehydration as they travel through seas with varying salt levels.

Fish owe their dazzling sheen to a pure form of the amino acid guanine. The substance, crystallized into tiny flattened plates and arranged in myriad parallel arrays, reflects light like hundreds of microscopic mirrors. The result is the familiar flashy silver appearance of the archetypical fish.

The precise placement of the guanine platelets creates optical interference in which some wavelengths of light are admitted and others are reflected. From this interference arises the magical interplay of hues on the skin of living fish. The effect disappears when a fish dies and drying reorganizes the platelets.

Crocodile Fish

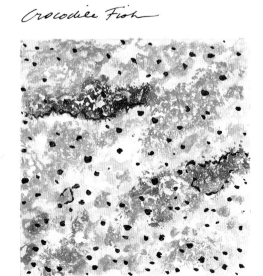

Lemonpeel Angel Fish

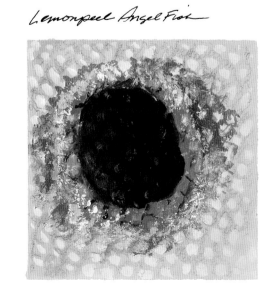

Japanese Angler Fish

ELECTRIC EELS, NATURE'S SHOCK TROOPS, ARE EQUIPPED WITH BIOLOGICAL BATTERY PACKS THAT CARRY ENOUGH ELECTRIC POWER TO LIGHT UP A DOZEN HOUSEHOLD LIGHT BULBS. ALL THIS CURRENT CAN KILL A PERSON ON CONTACT OR STUN A HORSE AT 20 FEET. A SINGLE 90-POUND SOUTH AMERICAN SPECIMEN THAT RESIDES AT THE NEW YORK AQUARIUM CAN KEEP HIS OWN ROOMY TANK WELL-LIT. THAT'S 650 VOLTS OF ELECTRICAL CHARGE!

TORPEDO RAYS HAUL POWER PACKS AT THE BASE OF THEIR PECTORAL FINS. THERE, THE MUSCLES FORM ELECTRICAL PLATES WITH A POSITIVE TOPSIDE AND A NEGATIVE UNDERSIDE.

ANEMONE FISH

MEMBERS OF THE FAMILIES OF DAMSEL FISH, ANEMONE FISH, AND CLOWN FISH LIVE IN HARMONY ON THE CORAL REEF.

TO PROTECT THEMSELVES FROM THE ANEMONE'S DEADLY STING, CLOWN FISH WEAR A "GREASEPAINT" OF SLIMY MUCOUS, AS THE ANEMONE DO AS TO PROTECT THEMSELVES FROM THEIR OWN STING TENACLES.

CLOWN FISH CAN AFFORD TO BE FLASHY. HOVERING CLOSE TO THEIR REFUGE WITHIN THE WAVING TENTACLES OF THEIR SYMBIONT, THE SEA ANEMONE, THEY FLAUNT WHIMSICAL COMBINATIONS OF NEON ORANGE, RED, BLACK, AND WHITE.

IN EXCHANGE FOR THE SAFETY IT OFFERS THE CLOWN FISH, THE IMMOBILE ANEMONE NIBBLES ON WHATEVER FOOD THE FISH DROPS. SOME SPECIES OF FISH ARE WARNED AWAY BY THE CLOWN FISH'S BRIGHT COSTUME, BUT OTHERS ARE LURED TOWARDS THE ANEMONE WHEN THEY SEE A FISH SO SAFELY NESTLED WITHIN. UNFORTUNATELY, THESE PREDATORS DO NOT SHARE THE CLOWN FISH'S IMMUNITY TO THE FATAL STINGS.

Breathing and Sleeping

Pity the poor fish struggling for breath! Water contains only about five percent of the oxygen available in air, plus it's a hundred times more viscous and a thousand times denser than our atmosphere. A fish may expend 20 percent of its oxygen supply just gathering more oxygen, compared with the one or two percent used by mammals. They pass enormous volumes of water over their gills — the respiratory surface — to meet their oxygen needs. Fortunately for the fish, gills absorb oxygen four to five times more efficiently than the lungs of most mammals.

Gills consist of filamentous tissue arranged in tiny parallel folds, called lamellae. Different types of fish have different kinds of gill coverings, which act as one-way valves. Water that rushes into a fish's mouth filters through the lamellae, which absorb oxygen and release carbon dioxide and gaseous nitrogenous waste. The water then passes out through the gill slits.

A fish in Peru's Lake Titicaca, the highest navigable lake on earth, has access to 20 percent less oxygen than a fish at sea level.

Tuna, mackerels, and sharks cannot stop swimming, for they depend on the current created by their forward movement to deliver water to their gills. Their double row of lamellae provides a respiratory surface up to 10 times larger than the surface area of their body.

Lung fish, a freshwater species, has a single lung; African and South American varieties breath by gulping air. By estivating, or hibernating, in mud capsules that trap air and moisture, they can survive for long periods of time in almost dry streams, or during droughts.

Taking a Breather from Breathing.

Functioning either as nocturnal or diurnal creatures, marine animals do rest, taking whatever shelter suits their taste.

By day, nocturnal corals at rest look like brilliantly colored rock formations. At night, they explode into a feathery forest of quivering polyps and tentacles.

$\mathcal{S}$LEEP FOR FISH SEEMS TO BE A LISTLESS STATE IN WHICH THEY MAINTAIN BALANCE BUT MOVE SLOWLY. BECAUSE FISH HAVE NO EYELIDS, THEY CAN USUALLY SPOT DANGER WHILE ASLEEP AND DART AWAY IF NECESSARY.

$\mathcal{P}$ARROT FISH LIE ON CORAL AT NIGHT, APPEARING TOTALLY COMATOSE. SOMETIMES THEY SECRETE, FOR PROTECTION, A GELATINOUS COCOON THAT COVERS THEIR ENTIRE BODIES.

$\mathcal{T}$HE PROTOPTERUS FISH RESEMBLES RIP VAN WINKLE WHEN IT ENTERS INTO A STATE OF ESTIVATION WITHIN A MUCOUS COCOON THAT OPENS ONLY AT THE MOUTH. ITS HEART BEATS ABOUT THREE TIMES PER MINUTE AND ITS BREATHING SLOWS TO TWO CYCLES PER MINUTE. IT CAN SURVIVE IN THIS STATE FOR UP TO FIVE YEARS.

Parrot Fish

Hearing

Sounds made in the sea travel almost one mile per second, five times faster than they do in the air. Raindrops strike the water's surface, ice floes groan and shift, currents collide, underwater avalanches and waterfalls crash and undersea waves the size of thirty-story buildings rumble. The chaos reaches a roaring crescendo when lava and steam erupt from undersea volcanoes.

Below the surface, often at great depths, channels of water sometimes transmit trapped sounds over great distances. Once, the sound from a six-pound dynamite explosion off the coast of West Africa was heard one hour later in the Bahamas. A blast near Australia reached Bermuda four hours later.

Add to the din a cacophony of sounds made by "the locals" as they go about the business of hunting for food, attracting a mate and frightening enemies.

Place a certain shrimp in a jar, and the snapping sound it makes with its oversized claws will crack the glass. Imagine multiplying this by millions of shrimp feeding at dawn and dusk.

The elastic, thread-like muscles that mussels use for locomotion make crackling noises.

Nassau groupers kept mariners of yore awake at night with a drumming noise that sounded like hollow logs beaten for a tribal dance.

Marine catfish in muddy waters produce a thumping that sounds like the hoof beats of cattle stampeding across the prairie.

The croaker fish of the Chesapeake Bay sings its courtship song by vibrating its swim bladder to imitate a jackhammer. Eastern toadfish make grunts like foghorns.

Not all fish make sounds, but they can all hear with inner ears located behind their eyes.

The piranha compensates for the poor visibility in the muddy Amazon River with an acute sense of hearing, which aids in navigation as well as feeding.

Spiny lobsters saw their antennae across their shells, creating a sound reminiscent of creaking of doors in a haunted house.

Sight

Filefish

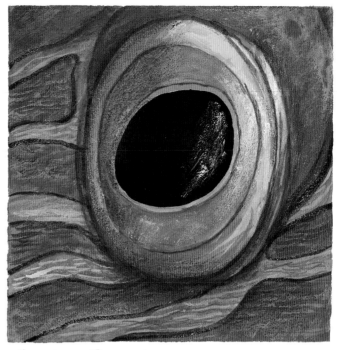

Saddled Pufferfish

Most marine animals are bilaterally symmetrical, with two sides that mirror each other. Except for the radially symmetrical coelenterates, all undersea animals, from the lowly flatworm to the decorative goldfish, have two ends — the head and the hind end. Marine survival depends on the ability to respond efficiently to stimuli in the direction of travel, which generally happens head first. As a result, nature has in most cases placed the sensory equipment for sight, smell, and taste near the opening of the mouth. The brain resides close by.

Most marine animals can detect light rather than precise form and detail. Some species have light-sensing organs that pick up shadows and movement only. They might be placed around the rim of the bell-shaped body of a jellyfish, on the mantle of a bivalve mollusk, or on a stalk that pokes through a spidershell's peephole.

In the murky depths of the sea the ability to see clearly has made squids and octopi the most successful hunters of all the marine invertebrates. The eyes of these cephalopods have the familiar features of the human eye — the cornea, lense and iris — but in the retinal area they have twice as many light-sensitive cells.

Most fish have eyes along the same lines as terrestrial vertebrates. However, the lens focuses an image by moving within the eyeball, rather than by changing shape when muscles squeeze it as in humans.

Visual adaptation is as varied as the range of habitat: the deeper the water, the dimmer the light, the larger the eyes.

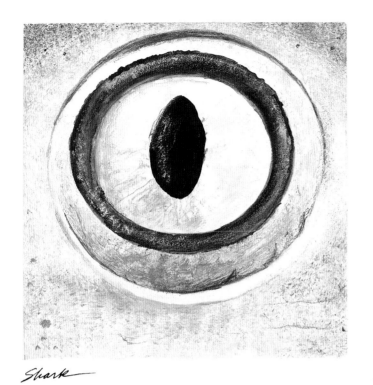

Shark

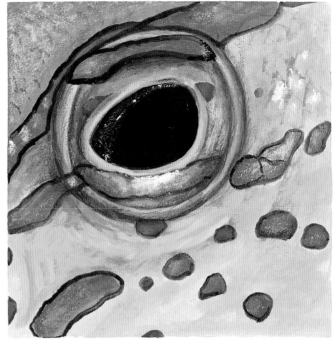

Multiopine Damsel

*I*NCREDIBLY, MORE THAN HALF THE INHABITANTS OF THE OCEAN'S DEPTHS GLOW LIKE LIVING FLASHLIGHTS. PHOTOBLEPHARON, FLASHLIGHT FISH, FROM THE INDIAN OCEAN HAVE POCKETS FILLED WITH LUMINESCENT BACTERIA BENEATH EACH EYE. WHEN THE FISH SENSES DANGER, A BLACK FOLD OF SKIN DROPS DOWN LIKE A CURTAIN AND BLOCKS THE LIGHT.

Moray Eel

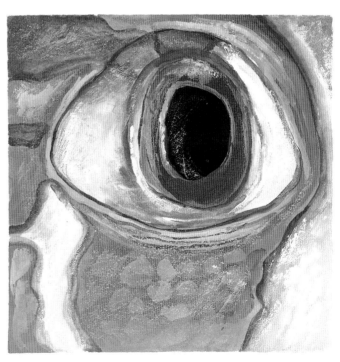

Tuskfish

Grouper

ISH, LIKE ARTISTS, KNOW THAT BLACK AND WHITE STRIPES MAKE A STRONG STATEMENT. TO THIS END, THEY HAVE DEVELOPED A FLAMBOYANT COLLECTION OF SNAZZY STRIPES AND SPOTS.

Catfish

Angelfish

Many-spotted Sweetlips

N'yasa Cichlid

Finger Fish

Clown Fish

Domino Damselfish

Moorish Idol

Cleaner Wrasse

Lyretail Molly

Defensive Tactics

Delectable sea animals have figured out many ways to avoid ending up on the menu. Flying fish can soar clear out of the watery hunting-ground. Anchovies form defensive masses so predators have a difficult time isolating a target. Eels and twinspot wrasse duck into protective crevices or burrows nearby.

The well-armored sea urchin is a living pin cushion covered with spines. Even the hungriest passerby thinks twice before taking a bite out of this oceanic porcupine.

Pencil Sea Urchin

$\mathcal{C}$HIRONEX, THE LACEY, DRIFTING AUSTRALIAN SEA WASP OR FIRE JELLYFISH, KILLS PREDATORS WITH A LETHAL PARALYZING POISON, WHICH IS RELEASED ON CONTACT WITH THE STINGING CELLS IN ITS TRAILING TENTACLES.

$\mathcal{D}$ARLING, YOU LOOK $\mathcal{D}$IVINE!

Spider Crab

$\mathcal{S}$OME MARINE INVERTEBRATES JUST WANT TO BLEND IN SO THEY ADD BITS OF THEIR ENVIRONMENT TO THEIR BODIES TO TRICK PREDATORS. THE "DECORATOR" CRABS HAVE MASTERED THIS ART OF CAMOUFLAGE, STICKING ORGANIC BAUBLES — PIECES OF CORAL, ALGAE, SHELLS AND OTHER DEBRIS — TO THEIR BACKS WITH SALIVA LIKE A NATURAL VELCRO. SOME EVEN ATTACH ENTIRE, LIVING ANEMONES TO THEIR SHELLS TO KEEP THE BAD GUYS AWAY.

PUFFERS AND PORCUPINES

PUFFER FISH AND PORCUPINE FISH, THE HEDGEHOGS OF THE SEA, CAN RAISE THEIR UBIQUITOUS SPINES FROM A FLATTENED RESTING POSITION TO MAKE A PRICKLY MOUTHFUL FOR WANNABE PREDATORS.

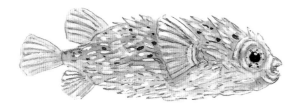

WHEN STARTLED, THE PUFFER FISH WILL BLOW ITSELF UP LIKE A BALLOON BY SWALLOWING WATER OR AIR. INFLATING ITS BODY INCREASES THE PUFFER'S INEDIBILITY, FOR WHEN IT DOUBLES OR TRIPLES IN SIZE IT CAN BE TOO MUCH TO SWALLOW.

TWO PUFFERS WHO MEET TO DISPUTE TERRITORIAL BOUNDARIES WILL PUFF UP AND FLIP BELLY UP, DISPLAYING A BRILLIANT WHITE UNDERSIDE THAT EXAGGERATES THEIR SIZE EVEN FURTHER.

Colorful Camouflage

Sea creatures dress for success in a world where safety is often skin deep. Masters of illusion, fashionable fish know exactly what to wear to coordinate with any habitat. Murky tones match rivers, marshes, and ponds; monochromatic schemes blend in the open ocean and cooler climes; neon colors go with coral cays; patterned costumes work in the dappled shadows of the kelp forest. Some colors last a lifetime, some change over the course of a lifespan, still others change at will. The only rule: don't look too obvious.

Sharks dress to kill in outfits of two-tone obliterative countershading. Their upper bodies are dark so they will look like water when seen from above, while their bellies are light to fade into the sky when seen from below. Phantoms in the void, the sharks prowl unseen, awaiting the perfect moment to strike.

Disruptive coloration makes the spotted triggerfish an entertaining escape artist whose psychedelic stripes and spots break up its telltale fish silhouette.

Predators can never be sure if the golden butterfly fish of Australia is coming or going. Another beneficiary of colorful disguise, it features a false eye spot on the rear of its cadmium yellow dorsal fin and a black strip that masks its real eye. When attackers mistakenly go for its tail end, the intended victim flees in the opposite direction.

The cobalt bands of the blue-ringed angelfish help identify him to his peers, while his white tail seems to vanish, disrupting his fishy form and confusing his enemies.

Because the upper waters of the sea absorb the red end of the spectrum of visible light, red or black creatures are effectively invisible in the darkness of the deep. Many red or black nocturnal species, such as the bigeye, the crimson squirrelfish, and the lunartail grouper, hunt by night in relative safety.

Cryptic coloration represents the ultimate achievement in marine camouflage. The creature armed with this tool changes color according to its mood. When emotion triggers certain hormonal and neuromuscular responses, its chromatophores — pigmented cells — switch to the hue that best serves the fish's needs at that moment.

Can a fish turn green with envy? Sea creatures can attract a mate, and express fear or aggression in all the colors of the rainbow.

Mimicry, another colorful survival tactic, produces schools of imposters and impersonators. Like a wolf in sheep's clothing, the stonefish, which carries a toxin that can be fatal even to humans, resembles the rocks of its rugged environs. The leafy-looking sea dragon mimics seaweed, turning off single-minded piscivores. And the gentle filefish has evolved to resemble the fierce puffer fish.

Most mysterious of all is the bioluminescence of aquatic animals that create light like underwater fireflies. Even at depths of 3,300 feet, a predator looking upward would see the silhouette of the lanternfish were it not for the counter-illumination emitted by the rows of glowing photophores on its underside.

EVERYWHERE IN THE "FISH-EAT-FISH" WATER WORLD, THE

BROWSERS, SCAVENGERS, AND FISH STALKERS (PISCIVORES),

SCAVENGERS, AND FISH STALKERS (PISCIVORES),

TO HOW THEY FIND THEIR FOOD : AS FILTER FEEDERS, GRAZERS,

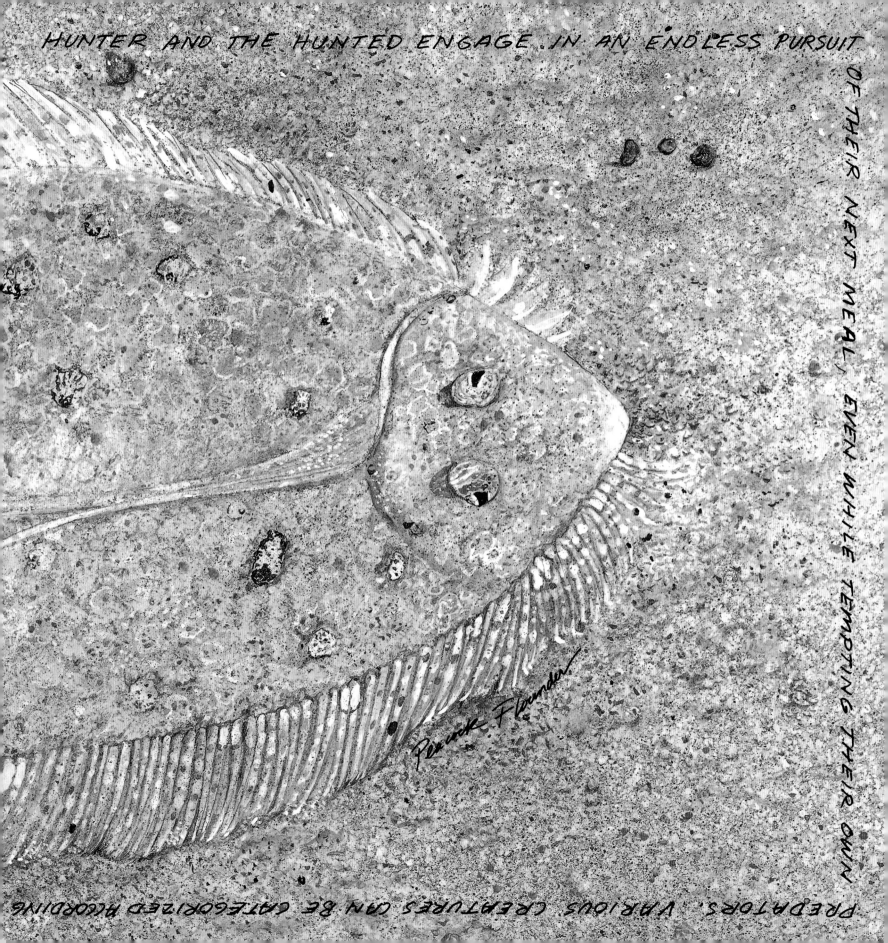

HUNTER AND THE HUNTED ENGAGE IN AN ENDLESS PURSUIT OF THEIR NEXT MEAL, EVEN WHILE TEMPTING THEIR OWN PREDATORS. VARIOUS CREATURES CAN BE CATEGORIZED ACCORDING

Peacock Flounder

Cuttlefish

Angelfish

Horseshoe Crab

Golden Seahorse

Cod

Goldfish

Sea Star

Marine Worm

Common European Crab

Porcupine Fish

Chambered

Painted

Snail

Red-legged Frog

Clown Triggerfish

Goldfish

ing Fish

Scallop

Blue Crab

Lobster

Bat Star

Shrimp

Armored
Sea Star

tilus

Weedy Horse

Tadpole

Squid

tle

Clown Fish

Coral

Snail

Flounder

Sailfish

Crab

Hydra

Rainbow Trout

IVER

"To trace the history of a river or a raindrop, as John Muir would have done, is also to trace the history of the soul, the history of the mind descending and arising in the body. In both, we constantly seek and stumble upon divinity, which like the cornice feeding the lake, and the spring becoming a waterfall, feeds, spills, falls, and feeds itself over and over again."

GRETEL EHRLICH, ISLANDS, THE UNIVERSE, HOME, 1991

The Riverbank

"*Eventually, all things merge into one, and a river runs through it. The river was cut by the world's great flood and runs over rocks from the basement of time. On some of the rocks are timeless raindrops. Under the rocks are the words and some of the words are theirs.*"

-- A RIVER RUNS THROUGH IT,
   NORMAN MACLEAN
   1976

RIVERBANKS LUSH WITH PLANT LIFE BEQUEATH A RICH SUPPLY OF MINERALS TO THE RUSHING WATERS OF THE RIVER. COUPLED WITH ABUNDANT OXYGEN DISSOLVED IN THE EVER-MOVING WATERS, THE NUTRIENTS MAKE THE LIFE OF A RIVER CITIZEN A GOOD ONE.

IN THE BOUNTIFUL RIVER, "UN PEZ GORDO" - THE FAT FISH, THE BIG SHOT, THE BIG FISH IN A SMALL POND - CAN THRIVE.

CRAYFISH PROLIFERATE, PARTICULARLY IN HARD, MINERAL-RICH WATERS THAT PROVIDE THE EXTRA CALCIUM THEY NEED FOR THEIR EXOSKELETONS.

$\mathcal{A}$ BRONZE BEAUTY, THE CRUCIAN CARP HAS ADAPTED TO THE TEMPERATURE, AIR, AND FOOD SUPPLY AVAILABLE IN STAGNATING PONDS, LAKES, CANALS, AND RESERVOIRS, AS WELL AS TO SLOW-MOVING RIVERS.

$\mathcal{P}$ORTUGUESE EXPLORERS CALLED IT O RIO MAR, THE RIVER SEA. FOR SHEER IMMENSITY, THE AMAZON RIVER HAS NO PEER: ITS VOLUME EXCEEDS THE COMBINED FLOW OF THE NEXT EIGHT LARGEST RIVERS ON EARTH. FISH ALSO GROW TO EPIC PROPORTIONS HERE. PIRARUCU AND PIRAIBA CATFISH, FOR INSTANCE, TIP THE SCALES AT 150 TO 350 POUNDS.

$\mathcal{L}$EGENDS ABOUND ABOUT AMAZONIAN PIRANHAS, NICKNAMED RIVER SHARKS. NO ONE DISPUTES THEIR VORACIOUS APPETITE, BUT ONLY 4 OUT OF THE 16 SPECIES POSE A DANGER TO HUMANS. ACCORDING TO THE GUINNESS BOOK OF ANIMAL FACTS AND FEATS, IN ONE EPISODE, A SCHOOL OF PIRANHAS ATE 322 OF THE 500 UNLUCKY PASSENGERS ABOARD A SHIP THAT CAPSIZED ON THE AMAZON. ALL THAT REMAINED OF THE VICTIMS AFTER THE FRENZY WERE HALF A DOZEN ARTICLES OF CLOTHING.

he Reef

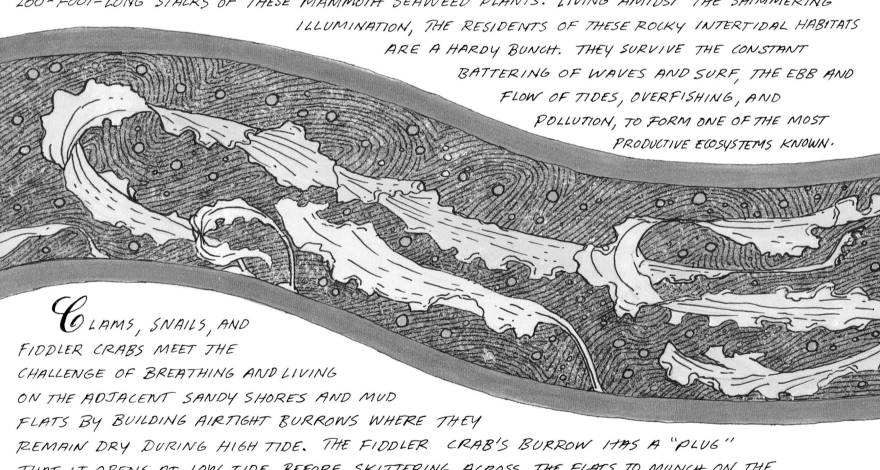

Fringing reefs formed close to the shore along rocky coastlines anchor cathedral-like kelp forests. Surface light reflects off the reddish brown or green leaves that sprout from the 200-foot-long stalks of these mammoth seaweed plants. Living amidst the shimmering illumination, the residents of these rocky intertidal habitats are a hardy bunch. They survive the constant battering of waves and surf, the ebb and flow of tides, overfishing, and pollution, to form one of the most productive ecosystems known.

Clams, snails, and fiddler crabs meet the challenge of breathing and living on the adjacent sandy shores and mud flats by building airtight burrows where they remain dry during high tide. The fiddler crab's burrow has a "plug" that it opens at low tide before skittering across the flats to munch on the organic debris left by the waves.

$\mathcal{T}$HE INHABITANTS OF THE CORAL REEFS REIGN AS THE PREMIER MARINE ARCHITECTS. ALTHOUGH THE REEFS GROW ONLY A FRACTION OF AN INCH EVERY YEAR, OVER THE CENTURIES THEY HAVE BECOME THE LARGEST STRUCTURES CREATED BY ANIMALS, INCLUDING HUMANS, ON OUR PLANET. THE GREAT BARRIER REEF IS THE LARGEST OF ALL -- OVER 1000 MILES LONG.

$\mathcal{C}$ONTOURED TO FOLLOW THE NEARBY SHORELINE, THE COMPLEX UNDERSEA CITY OF THE BARRIER REEF IS A TROPICAL PARADISE. ALGAE, SPONGES, MUSSELS AND REEF FISH, AS WELL AS VARIOUS VISITORS, ENJOY THE REEF'S FLOATING FOOD SUPPLY.

$\mathcal{Z}$OOXANTHELLAE, AN ALGAE, ACTUALLY FEEDS THE LIVING CORAL BY PERFORMING PHOTOSYNTHESIS AND RELEASING CARBOHYDRATES INTO THE CELLS OF THE CORAL. THE CORAL ITSELF SECRETES LAYER AFTER LAYER OF LIMESTONE WASTE UPON THE CALCIFIED REMAINS OF ITS ANCESTORS. WITH ITS MASSIVE, BEAK-LIKE JAWS THE RAUCOUS PARROT FISH EATS THE CORAL, THEN ELIMINATES THE LIMESTONE. THE PARTICLES OF LIMESTONE ARE GRAINS OF BEACH SAND THAT FORM WHITE BEACHES. A MEDIUM-SIZED PARROT FISH PASSES OVER A TON OF LIMESTONE A YEAR.

ave Dwellers

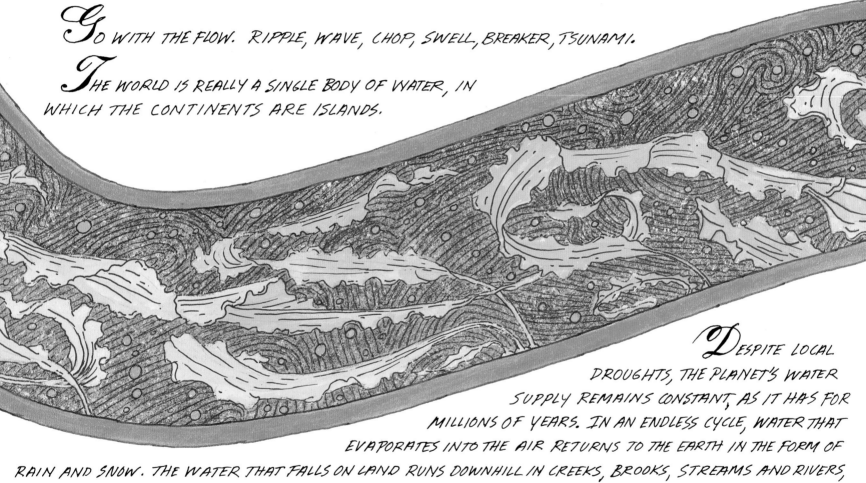

$\mathcal{G}$o with the flow. Ripple, wave, chop, swell, breaker, tsunami.

$\mathcal{T}$he world is really a single body of water, in which the continents are islands.

$\mathcal{D}$espite local droughts, the planet's water supply remains constant, as it has for millions of years. In an endless cycle, water that evaporates into the air returns to the earth in the form of rain and snow. The water that falls on land runs downhill in creeks, brooks, streams and rivers, to rejoin the great mother of us all: the sea.

$\mathcal{H}$eat generated by the sun's rays strikes the water's surface, releasing moisture into the atmosphere, where it condenses into clouds. Uneven atmospheric heating causes wind; wind creates waves and currents, both of which provide heat, transportation, and food distribution for the creatures of the oceans. The motion of the waters even helps species colonize new habitats, assisting in journeys that sometimes stretch thousands of miles across earth's largest "open space."

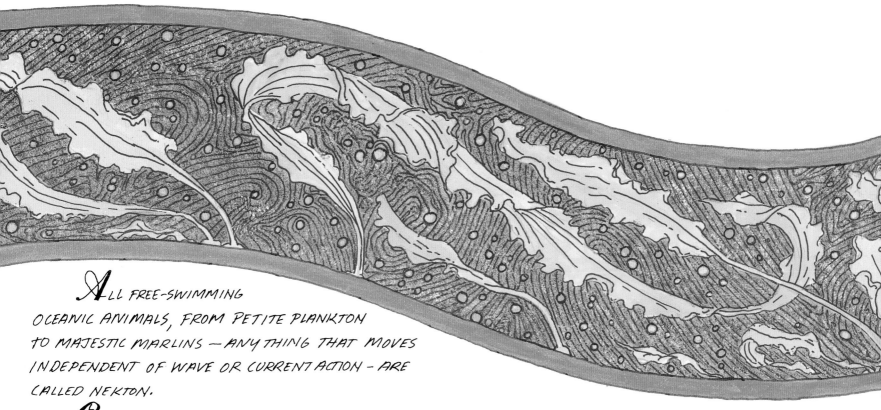

*A*ll free-swimming oceanic animals, from petite plankton to majestic marlins — anything that moves independent of wave or current action — are called nekton.

*O*pen ocean biomes, or communities, change dramatically between the surface and the abyss. This vertical layering reveals a fantastic diversity of abilities and characteristics that arise from variations in light and oxygen levels, salinity, mineral concentrations, water pressure, and temperature.

*I*n time, any poisons or pollutants created on land will reach the ocean's surface and filter down to its uncharted depths.

SALMON & SMELTS

*T*HE LIFE HISTORY OF THE ATLANTIC SALMON TYPIFIES THAT OF OTHER ANADROMOUS FISH, THOSE WHO MIGRATE FROM THE SEA TO FRESH WATER TO SPAWN.

*L*ARGER SPECIES OF SALMON, SMELT AND PIKE RUN UPRIVER IN WINTER WHILE THE SMALLER ONES WAIT UNTIL SUMMER. GUIDED BY SMELL, THEY OVERCOME NUMEROUS OBSTACLES TO RETURN TO THE STREAMS IN WHICH THEY HATCHED. THE JOURNEY, AS IN THE CASE OF THE PACIFIC SALMON, CAN COVER THOUSANDS OF MILES.

*T*HOUGH THE MALES ARRIVE FIRST, THE FEMALES CHOOSE THE SPAWNING SITE AND CLEAR IT WITH VIGOROUS FLICKS OF THEIR TAILS. THE MALES, THEIR COLORS HEIGHTENED, AGGRESSIVELY COURT THE FEMALES.

*T*HE LOVERS THEN LIE ALONGSIDE EACH OTHER IN THE NEST TO SHED THEIR EGGS AND MILT (SPERM), A PROCESS THAT OCCURS IN FIVE-MINUTE SESSIONS OVER THE COURSE OF A FORTNIGHT. EXHAUSTED, HAVING LOST 40 PERCENT OF THEIR BODY WEIGHT, THEY RETURN TO THE SEA. VERY FEW SURVIVE AFTER SPAWNING.

*A*T EACH STAGE OF ITS LIFE CYCLE, THE SALMON HAS A DIFFERENT NAME:

ALEVINS ARE NEWBORN HATCHLINGS;
FRY ARE LESS THAN A YEAR OLD;
PARR ARE OLDER BUT STILL IMMATURE;
SMOLT ARE ON THEIR WAY OUT TO SEA;
GRILSE ARE MALES MIGRATING TO SPAWN;
KELT ARE ADULTS AFTER SPAWNING.

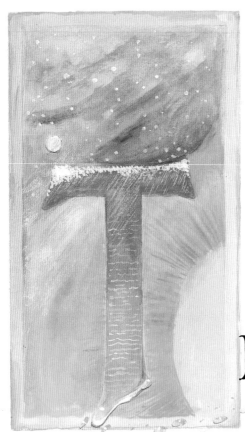

THE TEMPERATURE OF THE WATER IN MARINE AND FRESH WATER HABITATS CAN VARY DRASTICALLY. FROM THE SURFACE OF A PLACID POND TO THE ARCTIC DEPTHS OF THE OCEAN'S ABYSS, EACH ENVIRONMENT CHANGES WITH THE SUN, SEASONS, AND TIDES.

TEMPERATURE

FEW MARINE OR FRESH WATER ANIMALS ARE WARM-BLOODED, CAPABLE OF MAINTAINING A CONSTANT BODY TEMPERATURE; THE MAJORITY ARE COLD-BLOODED AND ADJUST THEIR BODY TEMPERATURE TO THE AMBIENT TEMPERATURE.

Warm-blooded and cold-blooded animals have developed a variety of mechanisms, survival strategies, which permit them to function at maximum efficiency to achieve the necessary balance between calorie requirements and temperature.

The colder the water, the greater the need for food to provide the necessary calories, but the smaller the chance of finding it. Many animals cope by migrating or hibernating.

Cold-blooded creatures such as crustaceans, echinoderms, and mollusks maintain their temperature when they cool by reserving their energy for absolutely essential functions like breathing. In a sluggish state, they manage to survive, though their hunting ability is greatly diminished.

Most of the world's 30,000 species of bony fish are cold-blooded.

Warm-blooded swordfish have large fat deposits in and around their brains and eyes, which is thought to act as insulation permitting them to dive deeply into deeper and colder water and continue to function.

Other warm-blooded ocean dwelling fish, such as tuna and billfish, have a mass of muscle attached to each eye which adjusts the brain's temperature as the fish plunge through waters with temperature variations as much as 60F.

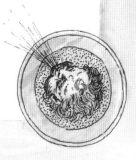

Migration

Marine animals migrate along well-defined routes, particularly when they seek to return to their breeding grounds.

How do creatures know when to migrate? What clues lead them to their destination? Evidence indicates that some of their tissue is light sensitive, and is stimulated by seasonal changes in the quality and quantity of light. Because of this sensitivity animals can respond to a change of season before the weather turns.

Some nomads navigate by observing the position of the sun. High-tech fish may use a kind of "radar" that is sensitive to the earth's magnetic fields.

Three impressive words describe the different kinds of fish migration: Oceanodromous fish, such as tuna, travel from one part of the sea to another. Anadromous fish like the salmon spend most of their life in the sea but return to their native rivers to spawn and often to die. Catadromous freshwater fish, such as eels, travel to the sea to spawn.

Copepods, the tiny crustaceans, know all about the ups and downs of life. They migrate vertically, moving up to feed at the surface during the night and dropping down (330 to 3300 feet) in the daytime. For a small, often microscopic animal, these are enormous distances.

# Eels

Looking For Love

From time immemorial European and American eels from the east coast have migrated, a phenomena recorded by Aristotle, among other ancients. These are catadromous fish, which means they live in fresh water but return to the briny seas to mate.

Each autumn, throughout the lakes and rivers of Europe and America, mature eels change their scaly costumes from (on their back) olive drab and yellow-brown to striking deep black and brilliant silver metallic sheen (on their sides.)

Garden Eels

$\mathcal{C}$LAD IN THEIR BREEDING ATTIRE, THE EELS SWIM TO THEIR BIRTHPLACE IN THE AQUATIC DESERT OF THE WESTERN ATLANTIC'S SARGASSO SEA. WHILE THEY MIGRATE, THEIR BODIES READJUST TO SALTWATER. FEMALES' SNOUTS GET SHARPER, THEIR EYES GET LARGER AND THEIR FINS BECOME MORE POINTED. THEIR OVARIES MATURE AND THEY CEASE EATING.

$\mathcal{I}$N THE SWISS ALPS, EVEN EELS FOUND IN PONDS WITH NO OUTLET MAKE DARING OVERLAND CROSSINGS, SLITHERING OVER DEW-LADEN GRASS AT NIGHT TO REACH STREAMS THAT CAN LEAD THEM HOME TO THE SARAGASSO SEA. THE EEL'S ARDUOUS JOURNEY TAKES UP TO SIX MONTHS AND ENDS IN SPRINGTIME BREEDING. AFTERWARD, THE EXHAUSTED PARENTS DIE.

$\mathcal{T}$HERE ARE ALSO EELS WHICH APPEAR TO STAY LITERALLY ENTRENCHED.

$\mathcal{G}$ARDEN EELS RISE FROM THEIR SANDY, TROPICAL BURROWS, SWAYING IN THE CURRENT LIKE THE EARLY SPRINGTIME STALKS OF A FLOWER BED. ALTHOUGH THEY ARE OVER A FOOT AND A HALF LONG, THEY FEED TIMIDLY ON PASSING PLANKTON, ONLY TO DISAPPEAR INTO THEIR VERTICAL BURROWS AT THE MERE SHADOW OF A PASSING FISH.

$\mathcal{S}$WIMMERS AND DIVERS, FORTUNATE TO SPOT A CORNER OF ONE OF THESE EXTRAORDINARY EEL "GARDENS", WOULD BE SURPRISED TO FIND THAT IT USUALLY EXTENDS WELL OVER 100 SQUARE YARDS.

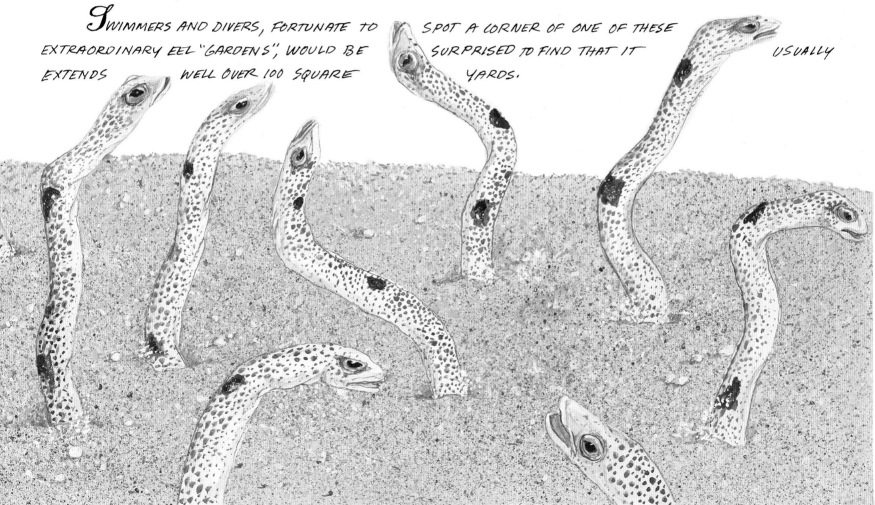

Getting Around

Many sea creatures would be bored by a couch potato lifestyle like that enjoyed by sponges, anemones and coral. Nor are they content to submit to the will of Neptune, like the passively drifting plankton.

Certain high-minded nekton-plankton have learned how to swim, quivering thousands of hairlike cilia to propel their single-celled selves about. Others, the flagellates, whip one long strand back and forth, pushing themselves forward.

Starfish, brittle stars, feather stars, sea lilies and other echinoderms feature sets of tiny hydraulic tube feet. These suckered appendages enable them to crawl across the ocean floor.

Among the mollusks, the colorful nudibranch, or sea slug, slides along on a trail of slime produced by the sole of its foot. Chitons use cilia to churn their way around, while other mollusks create propelling waves with muscular contractions.

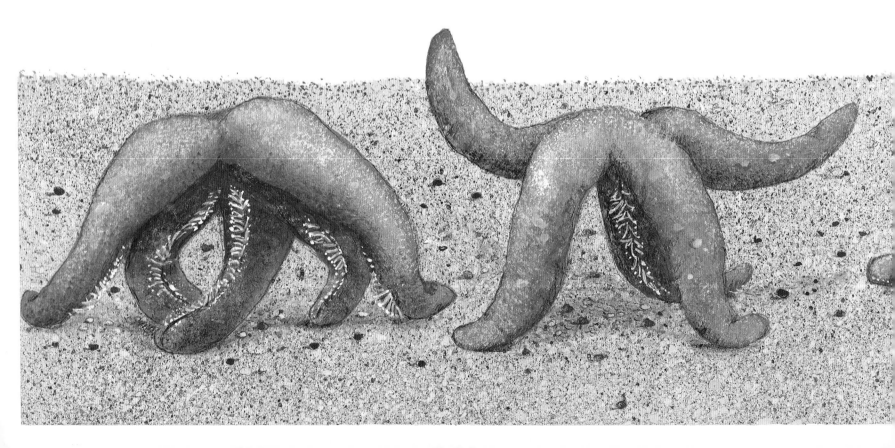

Rock oysters and mussels, who spend their lives attached to a hard surface, use their pseudopodium (false feet) for digging and burrowing. Only if their feet are well developed they can haul themselves along. Other bivalves swim by snapping their shells together like castanets, which creates a jet of water that propels them forward.

Crustaceans use only some sets of the jointed appendages located under their armored thorax, or torso, for walking. Feeling their way with their antennae, the ten-legged decapods -- lobsters, shrimps and crabs -- totter and scuttle about. Their other limbs, called pleopods, assist in swimming breaststroke-style. For a rapid escape, lobsters and shrimp can kick away with a flick of their hinged tail.

Whether in the close quarters of its lair or climbing rocks to forage for food, the octopus oozes fluidly along on its eight legs. This slow-motion water ballet gives way to turbo power in open water.

Like the octopus, the nautilus and cuttlefish can create a form of backward jet propulsion. It is the torpedo-shaped squid that breaks the invertebrate speed limit, drawing water into its mantle cavity before forcefully ejecting it.

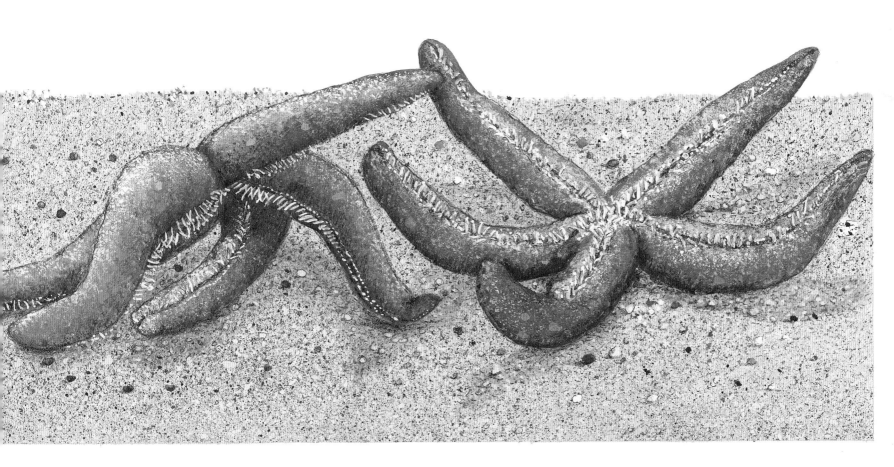

An underwater rock has started to melt and ooze at the sides like a candle that has become too hot. The mass moves down the side of a boulder and now changes color from a pebbly yellow to a blinding! white to a mottled brown tinged with maroon. Fantastic, unbelievable, weird --- it's an octopus.

Octopi

Squids

Cephalopods walk on their heads. But they do much more with that brainy globe, applying stealth and cunning to the task of surviving without the armor worn by other mollusks. Without a shell, they gain freedom, speed, and mobility.

When night falls and there is little light, squids use their ink to keep in touch with schoolmates and octopi use it to locate their mates.

The expectant octopi takes mother-love to sometimes a fatal extreme, passing up food and sleep to stand guard over the egg strands in her den during the months of their incubation. Despite her best efforts to ward off predators, only two hatchlings from a clutch of 80,000 eggs will reach adulthood.

Living fountain pens, these creatures come with their own pen and ink. A remnant of their prehistoric shell, the internal "quill" (the cuttlebone in a cuttlefish) supports their body. Bird lovers give cuttlebones to their pets, who groom their beaks upon them.

Cuttlefish

Cephalopod ink is the basis of sepia-toned India ink, which is used by writers and artists, but octopi and squid know better. They squirt clouds of the stuff behind them to serve as a smoke screen while they flee predators.

Sink or Swim

Swimming is not as easy as it looks. Even without obstacles and currents, the waterworld presents a unique complication: besides forward and backward, rightward and leftward motion, fish must deal with a third dimension, up and down.

Pectoral and pelvic fins help a fish control its pitch so it can rise, stay level, or dive. Dorsal fins permit the fish to roll on its own axis like a fighter jet. Steering, or yaw, to the right or left is achieved with a combination of fin angles.

Fish wriggle and undulate in a watery version of the twist to generate forward movement, thrust.

All rumors to the contrary, many fish don't quite float. Their body mass of muscle, cartilage, and bone has a greater specific gravity than water. To get some extra lift, some of the teleost (bony) fish use their swim bladder as a bouyancy device. The gas filled sac, part of the digestive system, regulates their internal pressure against that in the surrounding water so they can sink to lower depths or rise towards the surface.

When brought to the surface, inhabitants of the deep-water abyss explode. The average depth of the abyssal floor or plain is 13,000 feet. How these animals withstand the crushing water pressure of the deep remains largely unknown. One explanation may be that they do not possess swim bladders.

A HUGE OIL-RICH LIVER MAY HELP KEEP THE SHARK AFLOAT, BUT IT GAINS MOST OF ITS BUOYANCY FROM LARGE PECTORAL FINS HELD STRAIGHT OUT FROM ITS SIDES. THESE TAP THE PRINCIPLES OF HYDRODYNAMICS TO GENERATE LIFT, MUCH AS AN AIRPLANE'S WINGS DO IN THE AIR.

Pacific Electric Ray

*S*UBMARINES LOOK AND WORK LIKE A MECHANICAL KNOCKOFF OF A SHARK. A POINTED SNOUT AND STREAMLINED BODY MINIMIZE RESISTANCE TO THE WATER. HYDROFOILS IMITATE THE SHARK'S ROUNDED, TAPERED PECTORAL FINS TO REDUCE WATER FLOW, CREATE LIFT, OR SERVE AS BRAKING FLAPS.

Lesser Spotted Dogfish

*S*EA HORSES SWIM IN A DIGNIFIED, UPRIGHT POSTURE, PROPELLED BY A WAVING DORSAL FIN. STEERING WITH SMALL PECTORAL FINS AS IT GLIDES ALONG, THE DISTINCTIVE ANIMAL RESERVES ITS PREHENSILE TAIL FOR HANGING ONTO SEAWEED STEMS WHILE ON THE LOOKOUT FOR FOOD.

Smallhead Flying Fish

*B*USTED. FINE THAT FISH! SPEEDBOAT DESIGNERS DO WELL TO COPY THE FORM OF THE SAILFISH. THE CHEETAH OF THE SEAS HAS A SICKLE-SHAPED TAIL, SLEEK BODY LINES, AND A LONG, CRESTED DORSAL FIN THAT ALLOWS IT TO ZOOM ABOUT AT SPEEDS OF UP TO 60 MILES PER HOUR.

Flying Fish

The various species of bony fish known as flying fish literally take flight to escape ocean predators. Enlarged pectoral fins act as wings, allowing these fish to soar over the surface of the sea.

Shoals of flying fish break the surface at speeds of 20 miles per hour. Fluttering their tail fins in the water at high speeds can accelerate them to twice that pace.

In flights that last 30 seconds or more, foot-long flying fish spread their iridescent fins and glide forward up to one-quarter mile, a phenomenal distance considering their size.

The flying fish beats its powerful tail once again upon re-entry into the water to brake its speed.

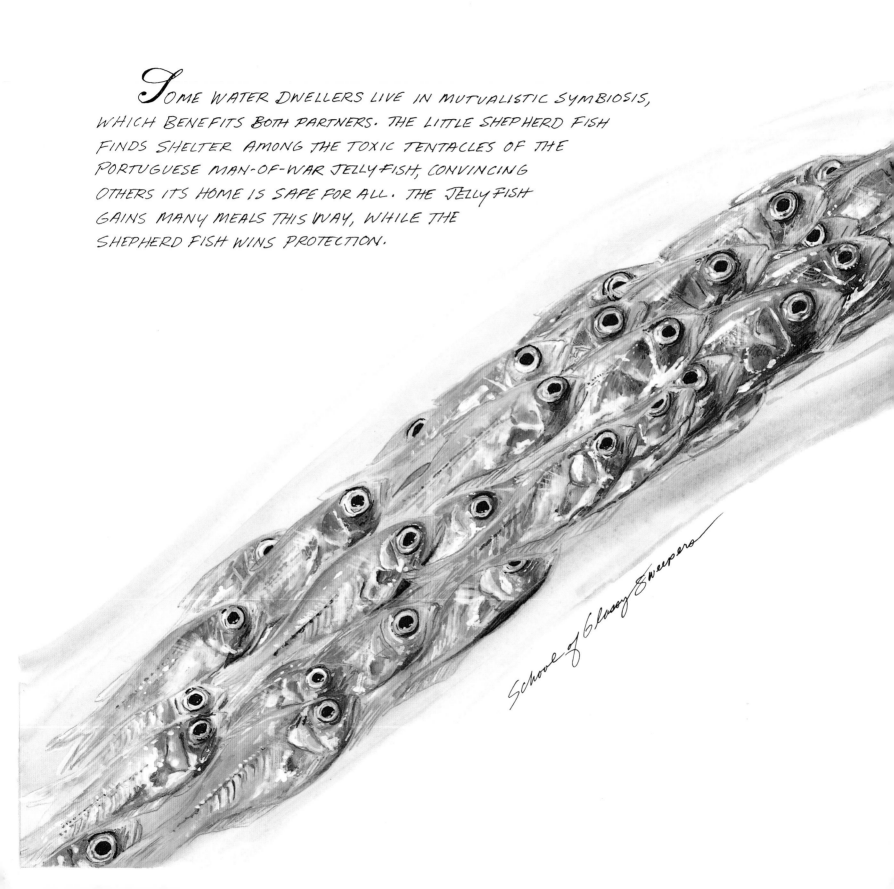

Some water dwellers live in mutualistic symbiosis, which benefits both partners. The little shepherd fish finds shelter among the toxic tentacles of the Portuguese man-of-war jelly fish, convincing others its home is safe for all. The jelly fish gains many meals this way, while the shepherd fish wins protection.

School of Glassy Sweepers

*F*ISH WHO LACK GROOMING-APPENDAGES AVAIL THEMSELVES OF THE SERVICES OF THE WRASSE, SOMETIMES CALLED DOCTOR FISH. EACH OF THESE FISH PERFORM A DISTINCTIVE ZIG ZAG DANCE IN FRONT OF ITS CHOOSEN "CLEANING STATION", ADVERTISING THAT IT'S OPEN FOR BUSINESS. THOSE WHO VISIT RECEIVE A THOROUGH CLEANING OF THEIR FINS, GILLS, MOUTHS, AND EVEN THEIR THROATS, WHILE THE CLEANERS FEAST ON ANY FOOD FRAGMENTS, BACTERIA, AND PARASITES THEY FIND. REGULAR CLIENTS LINE UP, OFTEN AT THE SAME TIME EACH DAY, WAITING TO BE PAMPERED.

*S*OME SMART FISH SWIM IN SCHOOLS, GROUPS THAT FEED TOGETHER OR FIND SAFETY IN NUMBERS. FOLLOWING VISUAL CUES AND READINGS FROM THEIR LATERAL-LINE MOTION DETECTORS, THESE GROUPS OF FISH MAINTAIN PERFECT GEOMETRIC ORIENTATION, THEIR BODIES ALWAYS PARALLEL AND EQUIDISTANT.

*T*HE RIGIDLY PATTERNED BEHAVIOR WITHIN MOST SCHOOLS REMAINS A MYSTERY, FOR THESE SOCIAL ORGANIZATIONS DO NOT APPEAR TO HAVE LEADERS. HOW DO FISH SORT THEMSELVES OUT BY SIZE AND GENERATION, AND WHAT GENERATES THEIR FLAWLESS CHOREOGRAPHY?

 EA

THE RETURN OF THE NATIVE

"*Who can say of a particular sea that it is old? Distilled by the sun, kneaded by the moon, it is renewed in a year, in a day, or in an hour.*"

THOMAS HARDY, 1878

WANT TO BE SCARED TO DEATH? IMAGINE SEVERAL GIANT MANTA RAYS ENGAGING IN A TERRITORIAL DISPLAY. DESPITE WING SPANS OF OVER 20 FEET AND WEIGHTS OF OVER 3,500 POUNDS, THEY SOAR AS HIGH AS 15 FEET OUT OF THE WATER AND LAND WITH THE EXPLOSIVE NOISE OF A DETONATING BOMB. BUT DON'T WORRY – BELIEVE IT OR NOT THESE MILD-MANNERED CREATURES RARELY ATTACK ANYTHING LARGER THAN A SHRIMP.

RAYS AND SKATES, RESEMBLING A CROSS BETWEEN A KITE AND A FLYING SAUCER, SOME FRIENDLY AND SOME LETHAL, FLY LIKE BIRDS THROUGH THEIR WATERY SURROUNDINGS.

EN GARDE! STINGRAYS REALLY DO STING, ELECTRIC-EYED RAYS CAN ACTUALLY SHOCK, AND SAWFISH RAYS MAY IN FACT, CUT.

SOME SKATES AND RAYS MATE IN MID-AIR; AND IN SOME SPECIES, THE FEMALES LEAP WHILE IN LABOR AND GIVE BIRTH TO THEIR YOUNG WHILE SOARING.

IN MANY ANCIENT CULTURES, PEOPLE ENVISIONED SEAS FILLED WITH MONSTERS. MARINERS FEARED A GIANT SQUID OR OCTOPUS WOULD DRAG THEIR SHIPS DOWN TO THE DEPTHS. ONE SUCH SEAFARER, THE KING OF NORWAY IN ABOUT 1000 AD, NAMED THESE CREATURES KRAKEN.

MONSTERS of the DEEP

Africa

"Sea serpents" sighted in modern times often turn out to be nothing more than enormous pieces of kelp that have detached from the reef. Their steady, sinuous motion, complete with a "head" that bobs in the water, evokes images of giant underwater snakes.

Supposedly a hundred times more poisonous than any snake on land, Belcher's sea snake of the Timor Sea, an arm of the Indian Ocean, is actually a reptile.

Nautilus

The nautilus is the only cephalopod that wears an external shell. Inside this shell lie many exquisite pearly chambers filled 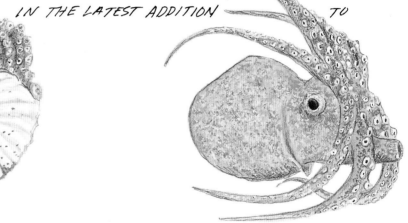 with a gas that helps the mollusk float. This sophisticated submariner controls its buoyancy by taking water into its shell and pushing it out. As the animal grows, it builds a larger living chamber outside its earlier rooms and lives only in the latest addition to its home.

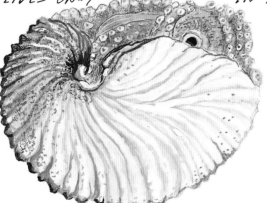

Paper Nautilus — in shell

Out of shell

In his book <u>20,000 Leagues under the Sea</u>, science fiction writer Jules Verne named Captain Nemo's submarine after the nautilus. A century later, naval designers tipped their hats to the cephalopod when they named the first nuclear-powered submarine <u>NAUTILUS</u>.

Long admired for the wondrous symmetry of a shell that represents a perfect logarithmic spiral, the nautilus increases its diameter by precisely three times with each complete turn.

The energetic nautilus has a lenseless eye and upwards of 90 tentacles. It can move fairly quickly and at night migrates up from the depths to feed on carrion.

Chambered Nautilus

SPONGES

Until the 19th century, scientists regarded sponges as plants. Found in all the seas of the world as well as some freshwater lakes and rivers, sponges live wherever the tide keeps them constantly submerged, for even the briefest exposure to air will kill them. Their habitat extends as far downward as the 27,000-foot depths of the abyss.

Any part of the sponge, if separated from the main body will grow into a new sponge. Since ancient times divers have cut sponges into pieces and secured them to the sea bed, where each piece grows into a large bath sponge.

Thornlike, barbed calcium carbonate spicules help support the sponge's body and discourage other animals from settling thereon.

Sponges conduct chemical warfare using toxins that make them poisonous to many tropical fish. Recent evidence shows these substances might prove powerful weapons against marine pollution, human bacterial infections and arthritis. Sponge toxin also makes a great shark repellent.

ANEMONES

*C*ORAL'S COUSIN, THE SEA ANEMONE GENERALLY LIVES IN COASTAL ZONES. THOUGH THEY RESEMBLE INNOCENT FLOWERS, THEY WIELD STINGING PETAL-LIKE TENTACLES IN A RING AROUND THEIR ORAL DISK. ANYTHING THAT VENTURES IN FOR A CLOSER LOOK WILL BE STUNNED AND DRAWN INTO A CENTRAL BODY CAVITY THAT IS ALMOST ENTIRELY A SINGLE DIGESTIVE GLAND.

*R*OCK POOL GARDENERS FESTOON THEIR WORKS WITH SEA BOUQUETS IN COLORS RANGING FROM IVORY TO YELLOW-BROWN TO PINK, REDS AND PURPLES. THE UNDERWATER BLOSSOMS CAN BLOOM FOR 50 YEARS OR LONGER, PARTICULARLY IN TROPICAL WATERS.

*T*HE BRIGHT PINK SAGATITA ANEMONE OFFERS SOMETHING MORE SHOCKING THAN ITS COLOR: IT HUNTS AND DEFENDS ITSELF BY SHOOTING STRINGS OF STINGING CELLS OUT THROUGH ITS MOUTH AND BODY SLITS.

NUDIBRANCHS

OR SEA SLUGS, FIT RIGHT IN ON THE REEF, A WORLD WHERE STONY CORAL TREES HAVE LEAVES THAT COME OUT AT NIGHT.
WHERE CRABS PRETEND TO BE WHAT THEY ARE NOT.
WHERE FLOWERY ANEMONES DEVOUR FISH.
WHERE FISH IMITATE SAND AND ROCKS.
WHERE DANGER LURKS IN BENIGN SHAPES AND FESTIVE COLORS. HERE, IT MAKES SENSE THAT SLUGS ARE BEAUTIFUL.

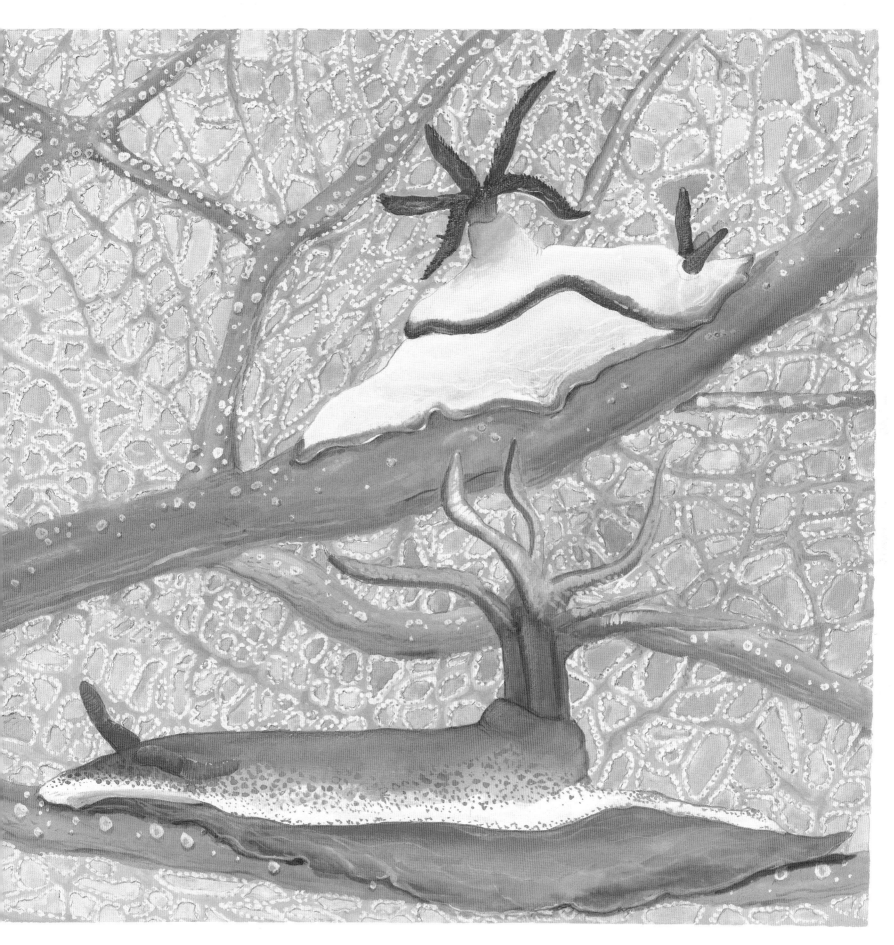

ANGLER FISH

ANGLER FISH GAINED THEIR NAME BECAUSE OF THEIR MODIFIED DORSAL SPINE, WHICH FUNCTIONS AS A LURE TO ATTRACT PREY. EACH SPECIES HAS ITS OWN VERSION OF A FLY, AND A UNIQUE CASTING TECHNIQUE.

DEEP-SEA ANGLERS HAVE A BULKY BODY, SMALL EYES, AND A POOR SENSE OF SMELL, BUT THEIR GLOWING "ILLICIUM" ROD HELPS THEM HOLD THEIR OWN. CURIOSITY SEEKERS DON'T REALIZE UNTIL TOO LATE THAT THE INTRIGUING LURE IS ATTACHED TO A FISH WITH A MOUTH FULL OF CURVED TEETH.

SOME ANGLERS CAST THEIR LONG LURE WITH A STYLE ANY FLY FISHERMAN WOULD ADMIRE, THEN REEL IT CUNNINGLY BACKWARD TOWARD THEIR MOUTH. OTHERS HAVE A STUBBY LURE THAT ATTRACTS PREY CLOSE TO THE MOUTH, SO THE ANGLER NEED ONLY LUNGE TO CATCH ITS DINNER.

I'll Never Let You Go

AS IF TO COMPLEMENT THE ANGLER'S BIZARRE APPEARANCE, NATURE GAVE IT A REPRODUCTIVE STRATEGY UNKNOWN TO THE REST OF THE VERTEBRATE WORLD. ANGLERS ARE SELF-FERTILIZING HERMAPHRODITES.

WHEN THE MATURE MALE SEEKS A MATE, HE SWIMS OUT IN SEARCH OF A FEMALE WHO GENERALLY OUTSIZES HIM BY TWENTY TIMES. HE ATTACHES HIMSELF TO HIS CHOSEN PARTNER BY CLAMPING ONTO HER BODY WITH A PINCER-LIKE JAW.

OVER TIME THE MALE FUSES COMPLETELY WITH THE FEMALE, DERIVING HIS SUSTENANCE FROM HER ALONE. HIS SPERM COME UNDER THE CONTROL OF HIS MATE'S HORMONES, WHICH TRIGGER THE SPERM'S RELEASE WHEN THE TIME COMES.

FEMALE ANGLERS OFTEN GO THROUGH LIFE WITH SEVERAL MATES AT ONE TIME. THE ANIMAL'S PHYSICAL FUSION MECHANISM HOLDS MANY SECRETS THAT SCIENTISTS HOPE WILL PROVIDE CLUES TO TISSUE REJECTION PROBLEMS FACED BY HUMANS UNDERGOING TRANSPLANTS. NO FEAR OF REJECTION HERE!

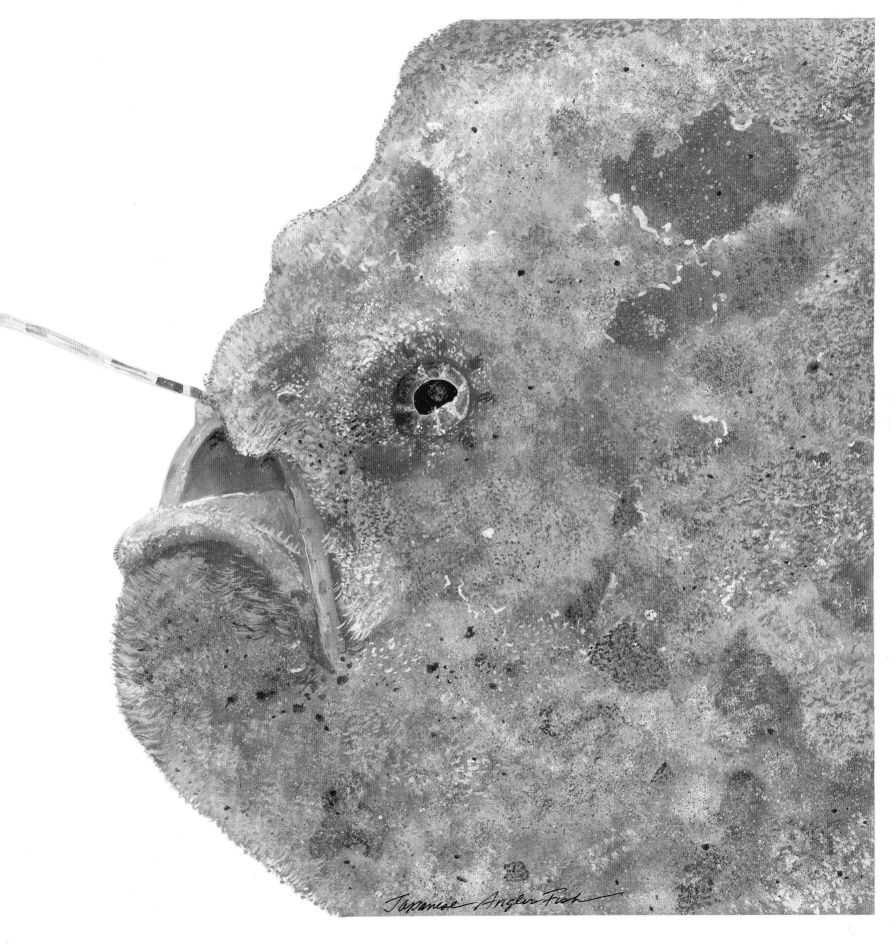

Japanese Anglerfish

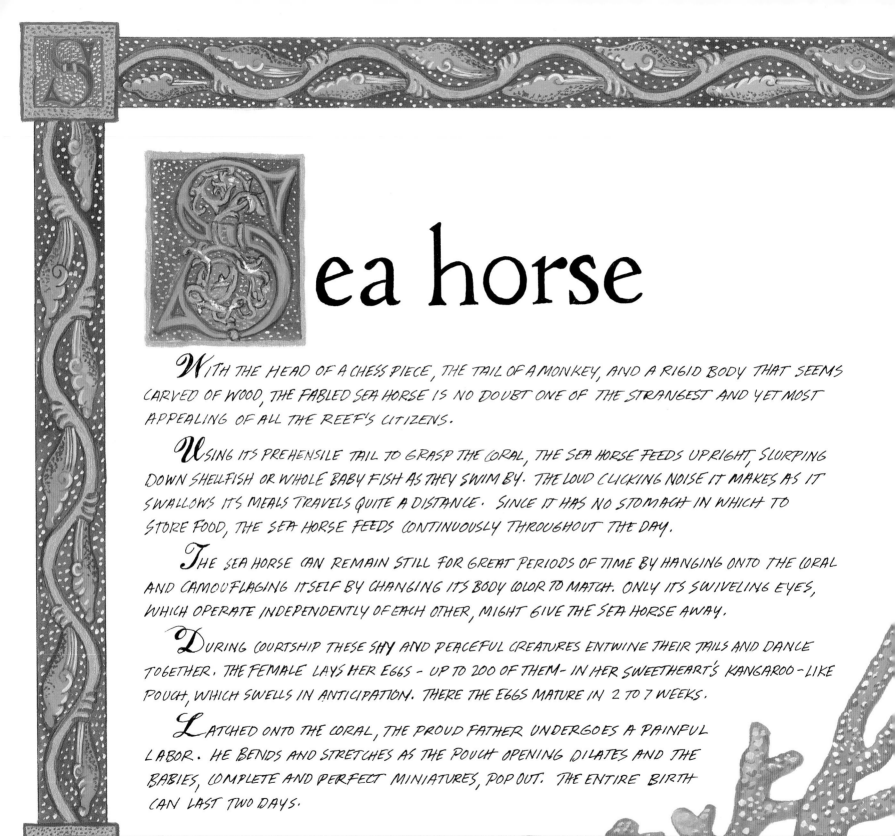

Sea horse

With the head of a chess piece, the tail of a monkey, and a rigid body that seems carved of wood, the fabled sea horse is no doubt one of the strangest and yet most appealing of all the reef's citizens.

Using its prehensile tail to grasp the coral, the sea horse feeds upright, slurping down shellfish or whole baby fish as they swim by. The loud clicking noise it makes as it swallows its meals travels quite a distance. Since it has no stomach in which to store food, the sea horse feeds continuously throughout the day.

The sea horse can remain still for great periods of time by hanging onto the coral and camouflaging itself by changing its body color to match. Only its swiveling eyes, which operate independently of each other, might give the sea horse away.

During courtship these shy and peaceful creatures entwine their tails and dance together. The female lays her eggs - up to 200 of them - in her sweetheart's kangaroo-like pouch, which swells in anticipation. There the eggs mature in 2 to 7 weeks.

Latched onto the coral, the proud father undergoes a painful labor. He bends and stretches as the pouch opening dilates and the babies, complete and perfect miniatures, pop out. The entire birth can last two days.

The aquatic version of a hummingbird, the sea horse propels itself with transparent dorsal fins that beat as many as 20 to 35 times per second.

Unfortunate ocean sunfish, rock fish and sea turtles with a taste for jellyfish succumb to an agonizing death when they ingest jelly look-alikes -- improperly discarded plastic bags.

ELLYFISH

Though they hail from Earth's inner space, jellyfish look more like UFOs from outer space.

Jellyfish have answered the complex challenges of their world with elegant simplicity. Supported by an endless waterbed -- they are themselves 97 percent water -- they need no bones or muscle. Like the snake-haired monster of myth, the Medusa jellyfish consists of a floating bell-shaped body from which dangle swirling tentacles. These appendages surround the mouth opening, ever ready to stun or kill prey.

Jellyfish have taken many forms as a response to varied lives. Those who call the dark mid-water home wear coats of many colors, while many from the sunlit surface are nearly transparent. Preferring the open ocean, most jellyfish live where few obstacles can damage them. Some, however, have adapted to the confinement of the pond.

Who's the biggest of them all? Simple: the Arctic lionsmane jellyfish. In 1865, one giant showed up in Massachusetts Bay with a bell-shaped body 7.5 feet across and tentacles 120 feet long. Its total length of about 245 feet more than doubled the span of a blue whale.

The adult moon jellies that appear in many of the oceans of the world during spring and summer vanish in tatters in the winter waves. But all is not lost: they leave behind a crop of tiny polyps that grow up into the next generation.

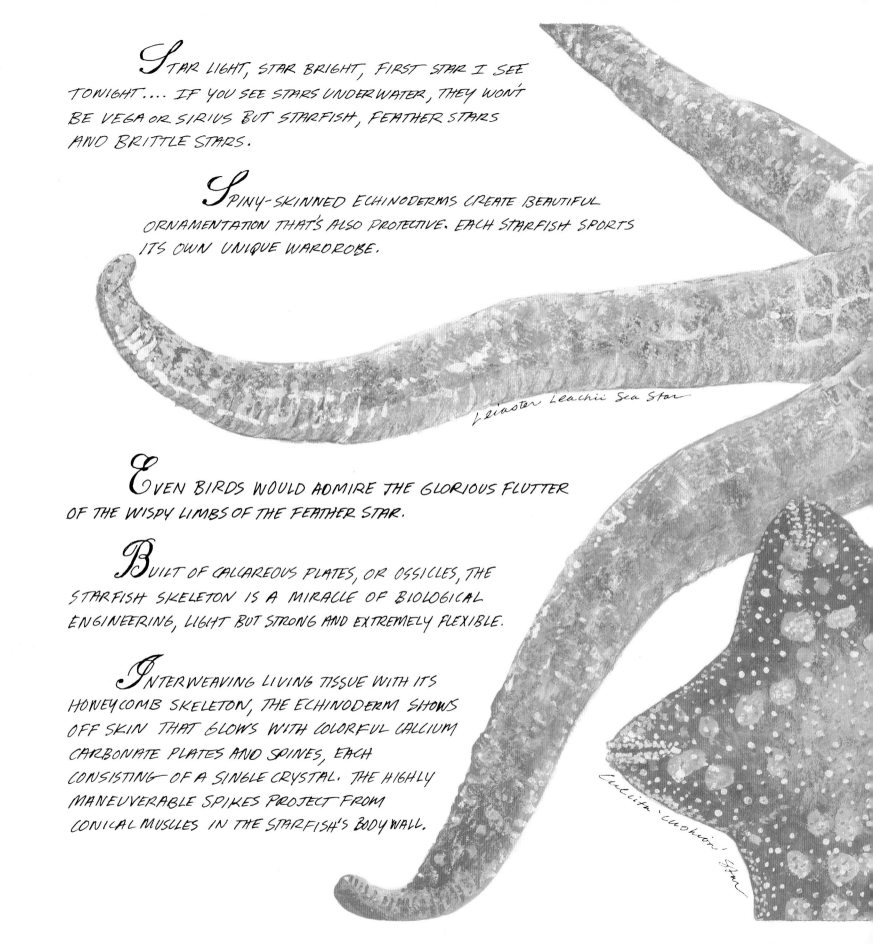

$\mathcal{S}$TAR LIGHT, STAR BRIGHT, FIRST STAR I SEE TONIGHT.... IF YOU SEE STARS UNDER WATER, THEY WON'T BE VEGA OR SIRIUS BUT STARFISH, FEATHER STARS AND BRITTLE STARS.

$\mathcal{S}$PINY-SKINNED ECHINODERMS CREATE BEAUTIFUL ORNAMENTATION THAT'S ALSO PROTECTIVE. EACH STARFISH SPORTS ITS OWN UNIQUE WARDROBE.

Leiaster Leachii Sea Star

$\mathcal{E}$VEN BIRDS WOULD ADMIRE THE GLORIOUS FLUTTER OF THE WISPY LIMBS OF THE FEATHER STAR.

$\mathcal{B}$UILT OF CALCAREOUS PLATES, OR OSSICLES, THE STARFISH SKELETON IS A MIRACLE OF BIOLOGICAL ENGINEERING, LIGHT BUT STRONG AND EXTREMELY FLEXIBLE.

$\mathcal{I}$NTERWEAVING LIVING TISSUE WITH ITS HONEYCOMB SKELETON, THE ECHINODERM SHOWS OFF SKIN THAT GLOWS WITH COLORFUL CALCIUM CARBONATE PLATES AND SPINES, EACH CONSISTING OF A SINGLE CRYSTAL. THE HIGHLY MANEUVERABLE SPIKES PROJECT FROM CONICAL MUSCLES IN THE STARFISH'S BODY WALL.

Culcita 'Cushion' Star

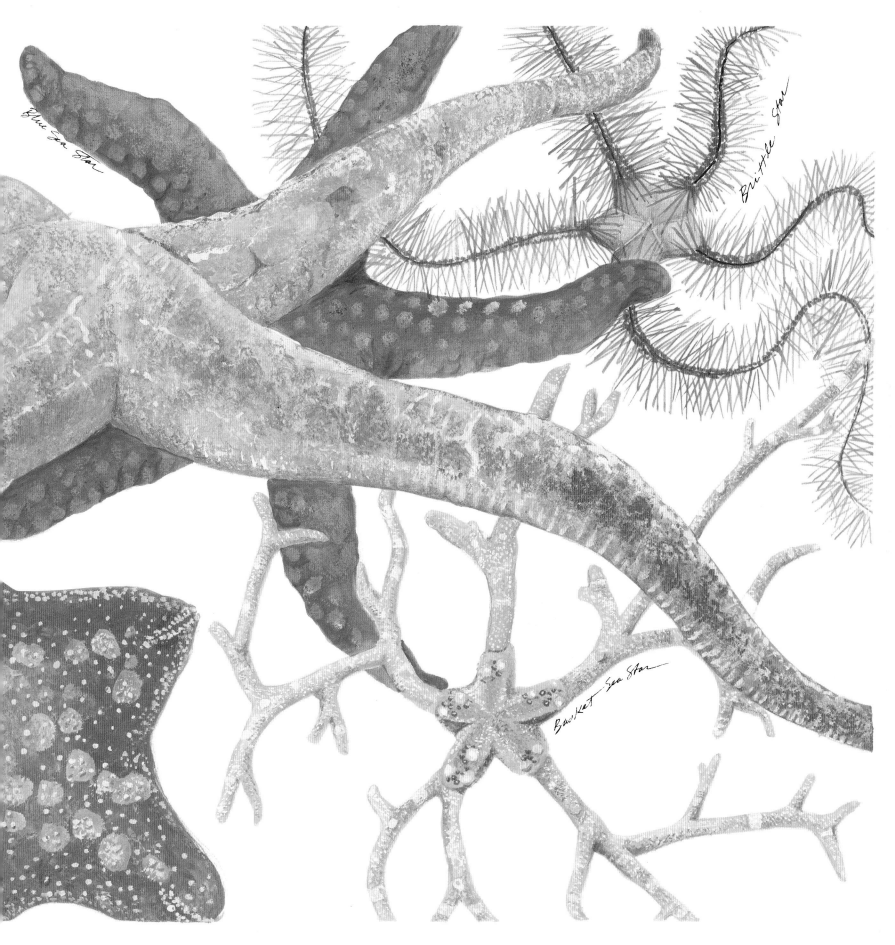

Blue Sea Star

Brittle Star

Basket Sea Star

SPIRAL SHELL

"*Human subtlety ... will never devise an invention more beautiful, more simple, or more direct than does nature, because in her inventions nothing is lacking, and nothing is superfluous.*"

-- LEONARDO DA VINCI

Leonardo's notebooks indicate that his double spiral staircase took its inspiration from the spiral columella of a univalve shell.

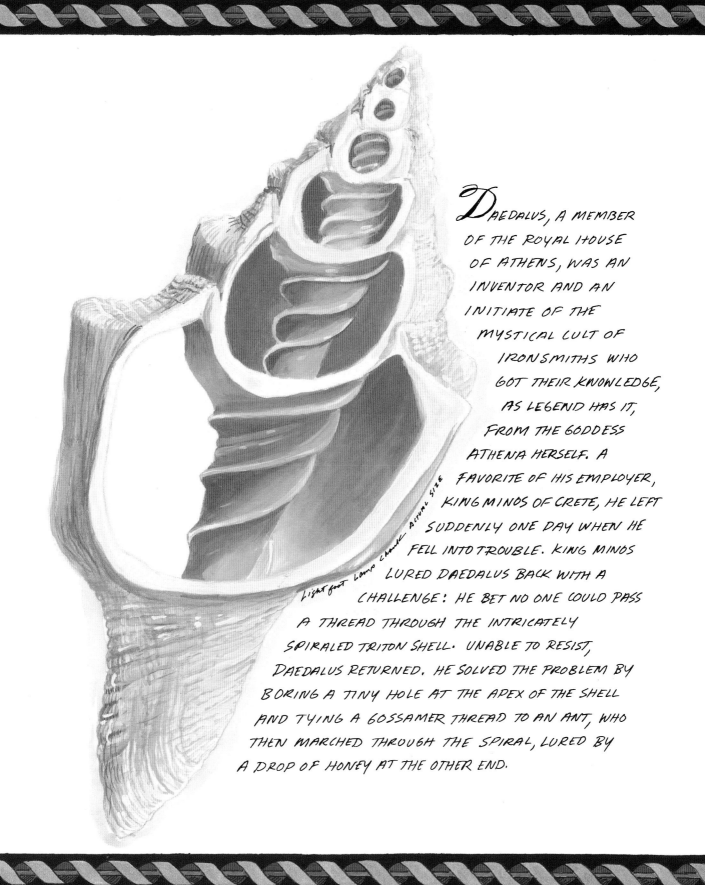

Light foot Long Chamk Actual size

Daedalus, a member of the royal house of Athens, was an inventor and an initiate of the mystical cult of ironsmiths who got their knowledge, as legend has it, from the goddess Athena herself. A favorite of his employer, King Minos of Crete, he left suddenly one day when he fell into trouble. King Minos lured Daedalus back with a challenge: he bet no one could pass a thread through the intricately spiraled triton shell. Unable to resist, Daedalus returned. He solved the problem by boring a tiny hole at the apex of the shell and tying a gossamer thread to an ant, who then marched through the spiral, lured by a drop of honey at the other end.

Auger

Button Top

Whelk

Hatchet Pyram

Oyster

Whelk

Madras Harp

Cowrie

Limpet

mon

Chrysanthemum Shell

Mussel

Trapezium Horse Conch

Glorious Scallop

Fig Shell

Crown

West Indian Fighting Conch

Chambered Nautilus

Volute

Queen Scallop

Coral

Conch

n cone

Spaced Oyster

Giant Melongena

Ivory cone

Bull Mouth Helmet

Mussel

Conch

COWRIE

*A*ncient reasoning concluded that an object that resembled a part of the human body possessed related magical and vital powers. Thus the cult of the cowrie was born.

*T*hroughout the world, the thoroughly feminine-looking aperture of the cowrie shell inspired belief in a wide range of generative powers: it was said to have been featured in the origin of the first woman and to confer fertility, protection against sterility, sexual potency, womanhood, easy childbirth, plentiful crops, resurrection, long life, medicinal magic, wealth, and safe passage to the afterlife.

*T*he cowrie also brought good luck and diffused bad luck, and in many places it was used as money. Ultimately, some of the magical powers of the cowrie were attributed to other shells.

Oysters Clams & Scallops

In western Scotland in days of yore, two people who made an agreement would split the shell of a mussel, cockle, or oyster. When the transaction was completed they rejoined the halves to signify mutual satisfaction with the deal.

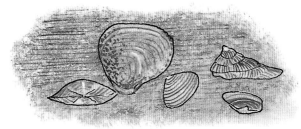

Asians adapted the closely fitting edges of the clam shell as tweezers to remove facial hair.

Wary of shell games? Consider this one: In Japan artists apply identical paintings to the inside of both halves of an oyster's shell. Several pairs receive different images, then the pairs of half-shells are separated. Half are placed face down, the others are distributed amongst the players. The player who matches up both halves of his or her shell quickest is the winner.

James Boswell, the 18th-century writer, tells us that the shells of swan mussels were used for skimming milk and serving shots of whiskey in the Scottish highlands.

Artists and illuminators throughout medieval Europe employed the shell of the painter's mussel to hold paints and liquid gold and silver while they worked.

For centuries the windowpane oyster of the Philippines substituted for window glass; some examples still remain in very old houses.

The ancient Greeks cast their votes in the first democracy by scratching the name of their choice on the inside of a mollusk shell, knowing that it could not be erased.

California Sea Moss.

Call us not weeds, we are flowers of the sea;
For lovely and bright and gay-tinted are we,
And quite independent of sunshine and showers;
Then call us not weeds, we are ocean's gay flowers.

Sand Dollar Sandwiches

serves: more than you might imagine
Combine one part sandy beach with
two parts salty ocean. Stir and scoop
onto sand dollar "bread" slices. Garnish
with kelp or any
found seaweed. Season
to taste with pebble
bits, crab claws,
or tiny
shells.

GOOD LUCK

$\mathcal{B}$EST ADVENTURES WITH A CHILD: BEACHCOMBING, SEASHORE STROLLS, PUDDLE JUMPING, A VISIT TO A TIDE POOL.

$\mathcal{S}$KETCHES, PAINTINGS, JOURNALS, AND PHOTOS CAN PRESERVE THE MEMORIES OF OUR VISITS TO THE WATER'S EDGE, NURTURING THE SOUL AND THE SOLE.

$\mathcal{F}$ORGET ABOUT PALM TREES AND PIÑA COLADAS: EVER CONSIDER THAT TROPICAL PARADISE STARTS AT THE EDGE OF THE WHITE SAND BEACH AND EXTENDS OUT TO THE BLUE HORIZON?

$\mathcal{F}$OR THE NATURALIST WHO PREFERS TO CARRY A FIELD GUIDE, WATERPROOF, PLASTIC-COATED, ILLUSTRATED DIVE CARDS FEATURE REFLECTIVE INKS THAT CHANGE COLOR ACCORDING TO LIGHT CONDITIONS AND DEPTH, FAITHFULLY MIMICKING THE CREATURES THEY DESCRIBE.

More About
Ponds, Lakes, Rivers, Seas

IN THE UNITED STATES:

AMERICAN OCEANS CAMPAIGN
725 ARIZONA AVE.
SANTA MONICA, CALIFORNIA 90401

THE CALIFORNIA ACADEMY OF SCIENCES
BIODIVERSITY RESOURCE CENTER
GOLDEN GATE PARK
SAN FRANCISCO, CALIFORNIA 94118

THE CENTER FOR MARINE CONSERVATION
1725 DESALES ST., NW
WASHINGTON, D.C. 20036

THE COUSTEAU FOUNDATION
930 WEST 21 STREET
NORFOLK, VIRGINIA 23517

THE NATURE CONSERVANCY
1815 N. LYNN STREET
ARLINGTON, VIRGINIA 22209

FRIENDS OF THE EARTH
1625 VERMONT N.W.
WASHINGTON, D.C. 20005

THE U.S. FISH AND WILDLIFE SERVICE
FISH AND WILDLIFE ENHANCEMENT
DEPARTMENT OF THE INTERIOR, ROOM 3024
WASHINGTON, D.C. 20240

THE WORLD WILDLIFE FUND
1250 24TH STREET
WASHINGTON, D.C. 20037

OUTSIDE THE UNITED STATES:

L'INSTITUT OCEANOGRAPHIQUE DE MONACO
AVENUE SAINT-MARTIN MC 98000

UNEP
UNITED NATIONS ENVIRONMENT PROGRAMME
P.O. BOX 30522
NAIROBI, KENYA

IUCN
INTERNATIONAL UNION FOR CONSERVATION OF NATURE
AND NATURAL RESOURCES
AVENUE DU MOUNT BLANC
1196 GLAND
SWITZERLAND

My DEEPEST GRATITUDE TO NATURE FOR ITS SPLENDOR, MYSTERY, BOUNTY AND GENEROSITY. MAY WE ONE DAY LEARN TO CHARISH AND PROTECT IT.

THANK YOU ALSO TO THESE INDIVIDUALS AND ORGANIZATIONS FOR ENRICHING THE VISION OF THIS BOOK:

TO MY FATHER-IN-LAW, DR. BERNARD KOCH, FOR HIS ENCOURAGEMENT AND PERPETUAL SUPPORT.

TO MY ENDURING PARTNER AND FRIEND, KRISTIN JOYCE, FOR HER CONTINUED CREATIVITY, LOVE, SUPPORT AND RIDICULOUS HUMOR.

TO SHELLEI ADDISON, THE UNSUNG NATURALIST AND CREATOR OF FLYING FISH BOOKS, FOR HER INVALUABLE RESEARCH AND TEXT THAT EMBODIES THE PERFECT AMALGAMATION OF BRILLIANT KNOWLEDGE AND QUIET INSPIRATION. AND TO CONSTANCE JONES FOR EQUALLY BRILLIANT TEXT EDITING -- AS ALWAYS.

TO THE CALIFORNIA ACADEMY OF SCIENCES IN SAN FRANCISCO AND TO ITS WONDERFUL STAFF, BUT ESPECIALLY, DAPHNE DERVEN, DIRECTOR OF PUBLIC PROGRAMS, ANNE MARIE MALLEY, COORDINATOR OF THE BIODIVERSITY RESOURCE CENTER, TERSA MEIKLE, LIBRARIAN, MAIN LIBRARY AT THE ACADEMY.

TO DON GUY, KRISTIN'S HUSBAND, FOR LENDING THE MOST REMARKABLE LIBRARY OF OCEANOGRAPHIC SOURCEBOOKS AND FOR HIS UNFLAPPABLE SUPPORT ON THESE PROJECTS.

TO OUR FORMER PUBLISHER, THE DELIGHTFUL JENNY BARRY OF COLLINS PUBLISHERS SAN FRANCISCO AND TO HER GREAT STAFF.

TO OUR EXCITING, NEW HOME WITH SMITHMARK PUBLISHERS AND TO THE CONTAGIOUS ENTHUSIASM OF OUR NEW PUBLISHER, MARTA HALLETT AND HER WONDERFUL EXECUTIVE EDITOR ELIZABETH SULLIVAN.

TO MY THREE CHILDREN, ESPECIALLY WENDY FOR HER EXTRA HELP, AND SUNNY FOR HER GOOD DESIGN SENSE. AND TO OUR FRIENDS AND FAMILIES, WHO CONTINUE TO SHARE THE OCCASIONAL AGONIES AND INNUMERABLE JOYS OF THESE PROJECTS.

Selected Glossary

Anadromous   Refers to the migration pattern of fish such as salmon that spend most of their adult lives in the ocean but move up rivers to spawn.

Bioluminescence   The production of nonthermal light by living organisms, including species of bacteria, marine invertebrates, and fish, resulting from the conversion of chemical energy into light energy.

Biome   Any major ecological community of organisms, including both plants and animals, which extend over a large area, and correspond to a particular climatic region, emphasizing the ability of living organisms to adapt to a wide variety of environments.

Cambrian Explosion   For four billion years only single-celled life forms existed on Earth. Inexplicably over the brief (by geologic standards) span of one million years, multi-celled animal lifeforms "suddenly" appeared during the Cambrian period, the earliest portion of the Paleozoic era, dating to about 570 million years ago. The Cambrian period obtains its name from the Cambrian Mountains in Wales where fossils of marine invertebrate species typical of the "explosion" were first studied.

Catadromous   Refers to the migration pattern of fish such as eels that live in fresh water and migrate to salt water to breed.

Chromatophores   A pigment cell in either plants or animals. In animals these cells contain mostly melanin, a black or dark brown pigment, as well as the less common red, blue, yellow or iridescent colors. The connection of the chromatophores to the nervous system in marine species permits the rapid color shifts, within   seconds, minutes to hour.

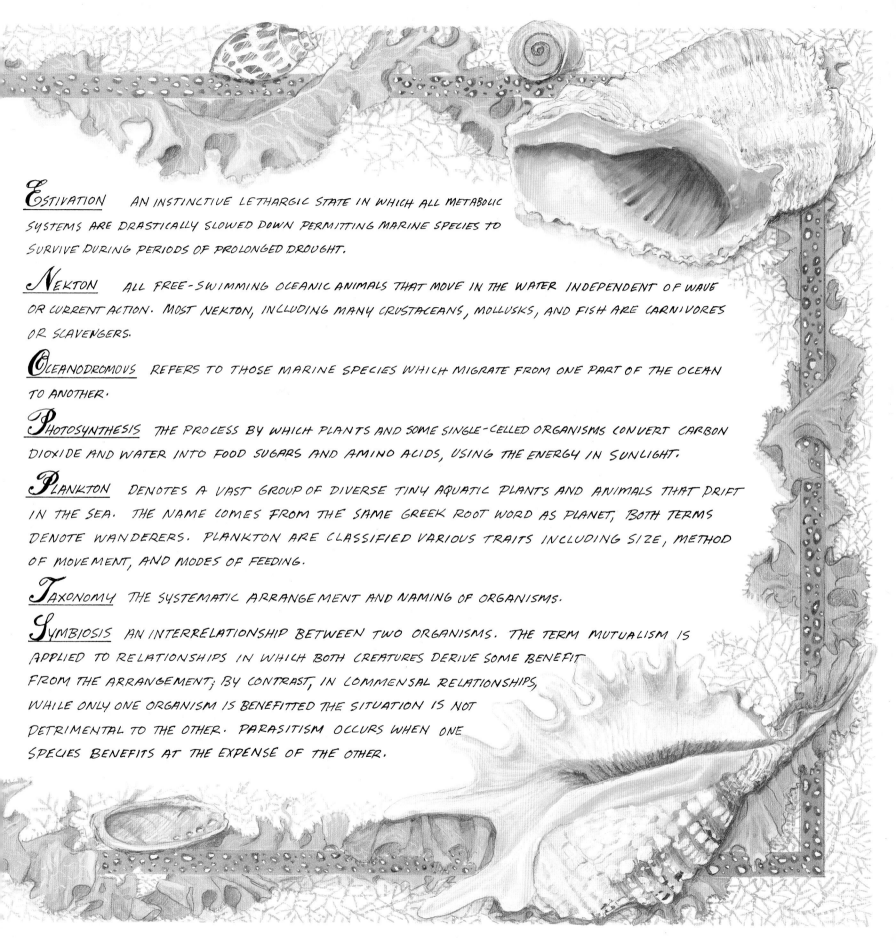

Estivation An instinctive lethargic state in which all metabolic systems are drastically slowed down permitting marine species to survive during periods of prolonged drought.

Nekton All free-swimming oceanic animals that move in the water independent of wave or current action. Most nekton, including many crustaceans, mollusks, and fish are carnivores or scavengers.

Oceanodromous Refers to those marine species which migrate from one part of the ocean to another.

Photosynthesis The process by which plants and some single-celled organisms convert carbon dioxide and water into food sugars and amino acids, using the energy in sunlight.

Plankton Denotes a vast group of diverse tiny aquatic plants and animals that drift in the sea. The name comes from the same Greek root word as planet; both terms denote wanderers. Plankton are classified various traits including size, method of movement, and modes of feeding.

Taxonomy The systematic arrangement and naming of organisms.

Symbiosis An interrelationship between two organisms. The term mutualism is applied to relationships in which both creatures derive some benefit from the arrangement; by contrast, in commensal relationships, while only one organism is benefitted the situation is not detrimental to the other. Parasitism occurs when one species benefits at the expense of the other.

Printed in Hong Kong by
Hong Kong Graphic and Printing Ltd.